WORDS
KIDS NEED
to
HEAR

Other Books by David Staal

Leading Your Child to Jesus: How Parents Can Talk with Their Kids about Faith

Leading Kids to Jesus: How to Have One-on-One Conversations about Faith

Making Your Children's Ministry the Best Hour of Every Kid's Week (with Sue Miller)

WORDS KIDS NEED to HEAR

to help them be who God made them to be

DAVID STAAL

ZONDERVAN.com/
AUTHORTRACKER
follow your favorite authors

Words Kids Need to Hear
Copyright © 2008 by David Staal

Requests for information should be addressed to:
Zondervan, *Grand Rapids, Michigan 49530*

Library of Congress Cataloging-in-Publication Data

Staal, David.
     Words kids need to hear: to help them be who God made them to be / David
Staal.
        p. cm.
     Includes bibliographical references.
     ISBN 978-0-310-28098-9 (softcover)
     1. Christian children — Religious life. 2. Parent and child — Religious
aspects — Christianity. I. Title.
     BV4571.3.S73 2007
     248.8'45 — dc22

                            2007034457

Internet addresses (websites, blogs, etc.) and telephone numbers printed in this book are offered as a resource to you. These are not intended in any way to be or imply an endorsement on the part of Zondervan, nor do we vouch for the content of these sites and numbers for the life of this book.

Interior design by Michelle Espinoza

Printed in the United States of America

08 09 10 11 12 13 • 23 22 21 20 19 18 17 16 15 14 13 12 11 10 9 8 7 6 5 4 3 2 1

To the men who attend Camp Paradise:
Make the end of your three days
the beginning of a new, incredible experience
for you and your child.
Worry less about what awaits you
on the other side of the river—
and more about what you'll take home
when you go.

CONTENTS

Introduction:

A JOURNEY

You will send several messages today.

Whether you intend to or not, you'll communicate thoughts, feelings, and beliefs to other people. And because the book you have in your hands has *Kids* in the title, some of those interactions are likely to involve children. Maybe your own. Maybe grandchildren, nieces, or nephews. Maybe boys and girls you work with in ministry, sports, or education. Whatever your role, ask yourself: What messages will I send to my kids today?

Estimates of adult vocabularies stretch to more than 60,000 words.[1] Throughout every day, I combine thousands of those words to form the messages I send. Too often, though, I don't carefully select which ones I'll use—they just flow from me like water streaming from a faucet. At times, they are nearly random. But with so many words at my disposal, surely I can do better. In fact, I am determined to do exactly that.

Why should I care so much?

Because relatively simple messages can make really big differences to children. And while some might seem unimportant and are forgotten in a moment, others will remain with us for a very long time.

I learned this lesson a few years ago at the memorial service for a friend's dad. All who attended listened to three adult children share their memories of a great father—and every memory included a specific message that had impacted that son's or daughter's life. They shared their late father's comments with details and passion that made you think they had heard his words just the night before.

As a father of my own young kids, two challenging thoughts entered my mind and have stayed there ever since: *Under similar circumstances, what would my kids say about me? What messages do I send them that will make a difference in their lives?*

My conclusion: If I'm going to say lots of words to my kids — and I will — then I should make sure I say words that count. And so should you.

I don't suggest something as unrealistic as scrutinizing and carefully planning every syllable of the thousands of words that we speak. We could never do that. Instead, I suggest something much, much easier — something that involves a mere handful of words.

After absorbing wisdom from mentors, soliciting advice from other moms and dads, observing parents who relate well to their children (and others who don't), reading books, and even asking elementary- through college-aged kids for their input, seven key statements emerged as the most important words kids need to hear. Yes, just seven. And in this book, each of those messages is assigned its own chapter. In my role as children's ministry director of a local church, I often suggest to parents that they make these messages a priority. As parents, my wife and I have used these same phrases for years. And now I am eager to share that perspective with you.

While these seven statements are simple to share with kids, you will find that they can make a profound impact on children's lives. Because they are also easy to forget, though, you must deliberately decide to speak these words. By making that decision right now, you can take full advantage of the remaining years of your kids' childhood.

An aviation-savvy friend once told me that a one-degree course change near the end of a flight could land a plane on the runway instead of an adjacent empty field. A one-degree course change at the *beginning* of the flight, however, will ensure that the plane doesn't just miss the airport but the entire destination!

Much of navigating the challenges of parenting also seems to involve relatively small course adjustments. However slight, certain changes can significantly impact the direction kids will travel through life. And just like the aviator's coordinates, parents' words can make the greatest impact the earlier they are used. Small messages, used over time, can lead to big transformations.

And that time is now because God has placed you on a mission to make a difference in the young lives he's sent your way. Regardless of your tenure — new parent, grandparent, or somewhere between — this book will help you make adjustments to the conversations you share with children.

And if you'll allow me to return to the aircraft analogy once again, consider this: when a pilot turns the wheel only slightly, the hydraulic systems magnify his or her effort, which causes large mechanical parts to move. The plane responds. Your messages, as small as they may seem, have a similar impact. To speak words requires little effort. But then any trust or respect you've earned, or authority you possess, magnifies their strength. And kids will respond. Of course you might not see that response immediately, but it will happen.

That's because messages matter — and this book will help you turn the wheel in the right direction. Notice that there's no claim that you'll become a super-parent. You will, though, make better use of your words.

First, let me offer some explanations that may add a bit of clarity to assist you as you begin reading this book. I'll start with a note about the language: all the concepts we discuss apply to boys *and* girls. Sometimes you'll read only "he" or "she." Unless tagged as gender-specific, you can assume that an idea relates to both.

Second, each chapter ends with a Big Question meant to challenge you. Resist the urge to plow past this tool. Take a few moments, a few hours, or even days to fully engage each question. Although the Big Questions are short, your answers will have far-reaching implications.

Third, while the book primarily speaks to parents, most concepts also apply to non-parent adults who have key relationships with kids. If that applies to you, one of the appendixes gives you a quick reference guide to additional action steps.

Fourth, the seven words and phrases covered in the pages ahead obviously are not the only statements you will want to share with your kids. These seven are messages for you to use in thousands of different ways over many years. Certainly, there are many more words kids need to hear from you — but these seven deliver disproportionately positive impact.

Finally, this book comes with no guarantee that your kids will grow up to become outstanding sons or daughters. Instead, a much more important objective is at stake — that your words will help them be who God has made them to be. Here's how that works: the messages you send your children can point them toward God or point them elsewhere. Whether they move into a full relationship with him is not a result for you to own, but a responsibility of yours to influence. So exercise patience and don't feel pressure to produce immediate results.

Instead, picture one day — maybe next month, maybe years from now — when your kids realize the difference your words have made in their lives.

Your journey toward that day starts when you turn the page.

"I Believe in You"

This is my Son, whom I love; with him I am well pleased.
MATTHEW 3:17

Say the word "camping," and you'll get a variety of reactions. Some recall hours filled with breathing fresh air, watching stars, and battling bugs on a back country, three-day hike. Others will conjure up a visit to the great outdoors in their recreational vehicle, munching micro-waved popcorn around a campfire before making a three-step escape back into air conditioned, bug-free comfort to watch a movie. In our family, though, camping is shorthand for two annual events: one week of father-son camp with Scott and one week of father-daughter camp with Erin.

The camp we visit, which our church holds each year in Michigan's Upper Peninsula, lacks luxuries such as plumbing and electricity. But that fact is vastly overshadowed by its abundance of bugs and stars. And life-changing lessons.

A Journey of Inches

On the first day of our inaugural father-son camp, my then-seven-year-old son, Scott, enthusiastically climbed a twenty-foot ladder to the high ropes adventure course waiting at the top. I reluctantly followed him, concerned over how quickly the solid ground I love so much fell further away with every step. The thin safety harnesses digging into my waist and legs provided a constant reminder about the fear I face whenever I battle gravity.

Once on the platform, I worked to hide my fear from Scott, from our sixteen-year-old safety guide, and from several fathers and sons who watched safely from the ground—that wonderful place I sorely missed. A light wind dried the perspiration on my forehead as I squeezed my face into a fake smile. Then that wind blew harder. The platform swayed. And I prayed.

The first leg of the ropes course required us to face one another, place our hands on each other's shoulders, and walk sideways on what resembled dual telephone cables. Loose telephone cables designed to carry calls, not people, I thought. With every side-step, we swayed. The more I tried to steady us, the more we wobbled. My cheap smile shrank, and Scott's fear grew, as did my feelings of inadequacy to protect my child. RV camping suddenly seemed so attractive.

Halfway across the forty-foot cable, Scott froze. He refused to go farther. He looked down, looked at me, looked down, looked at me—and, in a voice so soft that only I could hear him, said, "Dad, I'm too scared."

Oh, how I wanted to shout, "So am I, son. What on earth are we doing up here?"

Instead, I whispered back, "You're right—this is very scary. We can quit if you want. But I believe you can make it one more step because you've gone this far. Do you want to try?"

"You really think I can?"

"Buddy, I believe in you—you can do it. I'm sure."

Confidence overpowered fear as Scott slid his right foot six inches. "You're right," he said, and we inched our way to safety on the next platform. A mixture of cheers and tears erupted. Part of them were mine—for our safety, certainly, but even more for the words that had so unexpectedly come at just the right time, words that would mark the beginning of an incredibly powerful confidence inside my son.

My mind vividly captured that moment. Fortunately, so did another dad's camera. With computer-design help from a friend, I used the photo to create a poster for Scott that declares, "Bravery is when you keep going even though you're scared."

A couple months later, my family sat around our dining room table, enjoying a meal with neighbors. During conversation that jumped from one topic to another, Scott mentioned a career option he might consider: the military.

"You, a soldier?" one of the neighbor girls mocked.

Scott shot out of his seat, ran to his room, and came back with his poster.

"I'd be a *good* soldier," he said, "because I'm *brave!*"

Four simple words — "I believe in you" — whispered during a brief encounter twenty feet above the ground had redefined Scott's view of himself. That phrase gave my son the confidence he needed to move forward through life, even if just one small step at a time.

> Because when a parent believes in you, you begin to believe in yourself.

Why? Because when a parent believes in you, you begin to believe in yourself. It bolsters your self-worth. And self-worth matters.

Wobbly Steps and Long Strides

Every child needs to feel accepted and valued. He constantly wonders about himself and wrestles with competing self-perceptions — his abilities versus his inabilities. Ideally, the people closest to him will help tip the scales in this internal battle. When a parent or other respected adult rises to the challenge, the healthy self-worth this creates can help the child's confidence to blossom. The thought process works something like this: "My dad believes in me—so I should believe in myself." Sometimes the result is a wobbly step only six inches long. Other times, larger strides take place.

A child propped up by such confidence will face the inevitable challenges of life with resolve. Such was the case with Wilma Rudolph. Early in life, doctors told her mother that, due to a debilitating disease, Wilma might not walk again. Wilma decided to embrace a different prognosis. "My mother told me I would, so I believed my mother."[1] And that belief became the foundation that later enabled her to become a U.S. Olympic Gold Medalist in the 100, 200, and 400 (relay) meter races.

Words Defined

While the phrase "I believe in you" seems simple, let's take a closer look, because the message it conveys can actually be rather complex.

Kids constantly listen to their parents' views on a multitude of topics. Along the way, curiosity about what mom or dad thinks of them naturally arises as well. In fact, "What does Mom think of me?" or "What does Dad think of me?" can be one of the most persistent questions looming in young minds. And when the question is not answered to their satisfaction, kids can spend lifetimes wondering if they have mom or dad's approval.

In his book *Wild at Heart*, John Eldridge says that boys long to hear "You have what it takes to be a man."[2] Girls too need to hear they're making praise-worthy progress toward maturity—and receive parental approval along the way.

Fail to share such messages with a child, and he or she can grow up missing a healthy self-worth and looking for that elusive assurance from others. Instead, express your belief in a son or daughter early and often, and confusion can yield to confidence. Take it from Duke University's legendary basketball coach, Mike Kryzyzewski, who is a big fan of the power of "I believe in you." He says, "Those four words can mean the difference between a fear of failure and the courage to try."[3]

The sooner your son or daughter hears those four words, the better, because your belief in your child is every bit as powerful in elementary school as in college. Arguably, more so!

Phil and Gail saw this truth pay off with their sixth-grade son, Ryan. He tried out for a drama team, but didn't make the cut because he lacked important vocal projection skills. While he was disappointed, the setback didn't cause him to quench his desire to perform. Instead, only a few months later he boldly tried out for his middle school's spring musical—and landed the lead. Where did his confidence come from? When Gail asked Ryan what made him go after the role, he told her, "I believed I could do it because I knew you and Dad believed in me!"

Ryan's parents sent him the right message. A child will hear and trust "I believe in you" when the words feel authentic—in contrast to canned, overused statements such as "You're a great kid." Here's why: a platitude such as this—while well-intended—can sound cheap, impersonal, and plain too easy to say. In contrast, "I believe in you" communicates a parent's personal conviction and will last significantly longer in a child's memory. A kid like Ryan wouldn't benefit from hearing he's great—he needed to know someone sincerely believed in him so he could have solid footing to believe in himself.

Or put another way, hollow words can neutralize noble parental intentions. To prevent this unfortunate reality, psychologist Chick Moorman encourages the use of descriptive praise instead of shallow evaluation. "Descriptive praise describes accomplishments or situations and affirms the child rather than evaluates what he has done," he explains.

On the other hand, he says, in reference to mere evaluation, "When you praise someone with this type of parent talk [evaluative praise], you rate them with words like good, excellent, super, tremendous, fantastic, and superb.... Evaluative praise helps the person being praised to feel good *temporarily*."[4]

Do I suggest you stop telling your son he did an excellent job on his report card? No. But do continue on with comments about what you observed him do well, such as disciplined study habits or the numerous times he asked you to quiz him on spelling words. Should you avoid saying to your daughter that she is a fantastic girl? No. But do continue with specific reasons that build up to you conclusion. "Good job" and "you're great" as stand-alone statements deliver feelings that last only a moment Make your messages do more.

With that purpose in mind, let's seek to make the greatest impact with the words we say to children. When delivered clearly, without hype, and at the right times, the message "I believe in you" helps build lasting, personal confidence.

Words Put to Use — Two Important Questions

The late Fred Rogers once said, "Since we were children once, the roots for our empathy are already planted within us. We've known what it was like to feel small and powerless, helpless and confused. When we can feel something of what our children might be feeling, it will help us begin to figure out what our children need from us."[5]

Let's build on Fred's thought for a moment. We adults know what it feels like to accomplish something and wonder if anyone noticed or valued the feat. When a parent makes it a point to understand what his or her child likely feels in a situation — rather than simply focusing on the situation itself — then that parent gains an excellent opportunity to speak life-changing words.

So let's mix some practical strategy with Mr. Rogers' common sense as we observe our kids and discover how to share the words "I believe in you." Parents will successfully convey this life-giving message when they challenge themselves with two important questions: "What just happened?" and "What *could* happen?"

What Just Happened?

Every parent asks the question "What just happened?" after a loud crash or a younger sibling's screech of protest. Typically, those words mean someone's in trouble. For the sake of our discussion, though, let's set this reactive use for these words aside. Instead, let's put them into proactive practice by adding the words "that's worth noticing." Being on the lookout for "What just happened that's worth noticing?" will lead us to focus on and name specific, positive character traits in action — ones that merit reinforcement and belief. Prepare to exercise patience, though. All kids receive the seeds of character; some simply take longer to sprout than others.

But when they do sprout, we parents need to water them quickly with our positive observations. Failure to water a young plant can mean it will wither away—maybe even disappear for good. The same is true of these opportunities with our kids.

My wife and I try our best to capitalize on moments when we see our children display a fresh or emerging character quality. When this happens, we immediately look our child in the eye and offer a smile combined with simple words such as "Your kindness shows!" Many times we include a slight nod or hand on a shoulder. Sounds too simple, right? Maybe that's true—but it pays off. After years of this practice, we can communicate affirmation and belief in my son or daughter across a crowded room, simply with the nod alone. In far less time than you'll spend reading this sentence, you can send—and your child can receive—the message "I believe in you." The more you practice, the easier that will become.

In *Parents Do Make a Difference*, Michael Borba lists several easy ways to say "I believe in you!"[6]

I knew you could do it!	Every day you improve!
You almost have it.	That's a great idea.
You're doing much better.	You're doing a great job.
That's better than ever.	You must have practiced!
You're on the right track now.	

These ideas work the best when they immediately follow a child's actions, leaving no doubt in him or her as to what you are referring to. If time goes by, then a parent must make specific reference to the reason for the words. For example, "You know when you asked Debbie if she wanted to swim with you and your friends? I think you're doing a wonderful job making sure people don't get left out and have their feelings hurt."

Or take the compliment I recently emailed to the dad of a little girl I had interacted with at church, telling him he had good reason to be proud of this confident young lady. Since significant time (at least a day) had gone by before he received my message, for him to simply praise his daughter for her self-assurance when speaking with adults would mystify his daughter. To be effective, his comments would have to include a reference to the reason for his comment, as in, "Mr. Staal told me that you looked him in the eye and shared a funny story with him, and then said, 'Have a great day!' at the end of your conversation."

For such a passed-along compliment to have maximum value, it should also include the parent's reaction to the compliment. "Mr. Staal believes that you ..." delivers far less impact than "From what Mr. Staal had to say, I can see that you ..." Make the message personal, and you provide your child with a building block for her self-worth.

The challenge, of course, is to find these important opportunities within the context of your child's everyday life. The following three approaches to this discovery process can be a great place to start.

Slow down to look and listen. Life happens fast. So while engaged in activities with your child, or when simply observing her, suspend your attention on what is taking place and intentionally focus on who she is. What is she doing or saying worth noticing? Hint: noticing a child's efforts will provide you with better, more abundant fodder than waiting for accomplishments.

A parent recently described the benefit of paying attention to the journey his daughter traveled as she earned straight A's on a report card. Yes, high grades deserve congratulations. This dad described how her eyes beam brightest, though, whenever he tells her that he notices all the extra time and effort she puts in to her homework—and that her willingness to work hard might even be

> Anyone can compliment good grades at the end of a semester. I'm glad I didn't miss the real success that happened every night along the way.

her greatest strength. "My family knows I'm busy. But after dinner each evening, I'm real intentional to help the kids with their studies," he says. "Anyone can compliment good grades at the end of a semester. I'm glad I didn't miss the real success that happened every night along the way."

To look and listen for opportunities to speak encouraging words requires a parent who willingly slows down from the high speed of life; efforts worth noticing then become far more obvious.

Encourage your child's strengths. For some reason, it seems very easy for us to recognize one another's weaknesses. Unfortunately, this ability accomplishes little for parents when compared with what can happen when they encourage their child's strong areas. Throughout his book *The One Thing You Need to Know*, author and leadership expert Marcus Buckingham explains how development happens best through building upon strengths rather than constantly correcting weaknesses: a golden parenting tip.[7]

I once saw a young boy named Matt changed in an instant by an encouraging comment that took place along a river during one very hot camp afternoon.

You see, at our camp, although the water trampoline, weeds, and leeches provide big fun, nothing quite matches the river rope swing. Serious exhilaration takes place when your feet leave the platform as your hands clutch a thick rope, and momentum swings you out over deep water. Then fear kicks in when you must let go of that rope and fall toward the water like a shot duck.

Unfortunately, on each of his turns Matt released the rope too early and landed in shallow water. Several people, even his dad, informed Matt about his error. Repeatedly, they shouted, "You're letting go too soon." On his sixth try, Matt heard from his dad, "C'mon, what's your problem? If you don't do it right this time, this will be your last try."

Standing in ninety degree heat, the young boy froze.

So another dad climbed onto the platform and asked him if he knew what to do. "Not really," he whispered.

"Just hold on to the rope until you hear me yell 'Now!' and then let go," he said. "I've seen how strong you are, so this will be pretty easy for you."

Matt swung out, achieved great height, responded to the cue, made a big splash, heard cheers, and beamed with new confidence.

Later that night, his dad asked the other father what he had said to Matt. He had never seen his son so confident with something

new. The man who coached Matt replied, "I just told him what to do and why I believed he could do it, rather than telling him what not to do."

That counsel might sound simple, but don't underestimate the challenge. It takes little or no parenting skill to point out a child's weaknesses or mistakes. Instead, kids need adults who can identify and encourage their strengths.

Ask other people for help. After that interaction, Matt's dad became an affirmation machine. But first, he took a big, risky step — he asked other fathers what further strengths they saw in his son. Ask your child's teacher similar questions. Ask his or her Sunday school teacher or small group leader. Try parents of friends. Preface the question with why you ask: "I'm trying to focus on his strengths these days. Have you noticed something in him I could encourage?" That parent will likely give you an answer and maybe even ask you for your observations on how to do the same with his or her own children.

Before you share another person's comments with your child, though, try to observe the strong point or recall when you've seen it in action. Then you can enhance your comment with your own personal observation. Your child will appreciate that you noticed.

What Could Happen?

The message "I believe in you" can serve as needed affirmation today and an investment in a more confident tomorrow. Imagine the new leaps of faith Matt might now eagerly take.

One of my favorite illustrations of this principle comes from Ben Zander, conductor of Boston Philharmonic Orchestra and a professor at the New England Conservatory of Music. He believes grand potential is released when belief replaces the reasons for self-doubt, which is why he gives all his students the grade of "A" at the *beginning* of the course. Their first assignment is to write him a letter, dated at the end of the term, which explains the story of what the student will have done to earn this high mark. His philosophy: "This A is not an expectation to live up to, but a possibility to live into."[8]

Give your child an A and watch him or her live into the possibilities you've inspired. And begin to develop four new habits that can contribute to your success.

Articulate faith in your child. The well-known Nobel-Prize-winning-author Toni Morrison says, "Long before I was a success, my parents made me feel like I could be one."[9] Her observation is a powerful one—and one we can put to use with kids of all ages.

It came up one day over lunch with my friend and mentor Dick. I asked him what advice he had for me about raising a teenager—after all, my son's thirteenth birthday was quickly approaching, and I'd heard that parenting challenges change when the teen years arrive. "Expect the best from him, and tell him that you do," Dick said. "Then watch him chase it to make it happen."

Then Dick got more specific. "For instance, many parents joke about how awful they expect their children to be as drivers. Your son as a driver might seem a long ways off, but it's not. So instead of making light of him, take any opportunity you have to tell your son that you believe he'll make an excellent driver some day, and give him a reason or two why. Take that same logic about predicting his success and apply it to as many situations as you can."

Look for opportunities to increase trust in your child. These opportunities occur as your child steps up and handles responsibilities and challenging situations.

One Saturday afternoon, a dad in our neighborhood stood and watched his nine-year-old son mow the yard. His lines were crooked — to be expected from someone not much taller than the mower's handles. But the dad resisted the urge to take over or continually correct him. Our mailman, Anthony, happened to walk by and summed up the situation well: "Looks like there's something important growing in your yard."

The chances for you to demonstrate trust in your child are everywhere. A kid can clean the windows while you pump gas, order lunch and clear the table at a restaurant (if you, like us, typically eat at places without bus staff!), or volunteer at church alongside you. Let your son or daughter handle the opportunity with as little repeated instruction from you as possible, and he or she will feel your trust. Keep in mind that there's more at stake than just the work at hand, so care more about the child's growth than about straight lines or smear-free windows.

Express steadfast belief in your child when you're both in front of other people. Some parents avoid doing this, for fear they'll come across as a braggart — a legitimate concern when the child isn't present or if the comments involve exaggeration. But when a kid is nearby enough to hear your words — go ahead and brag a little. There's much to gain. To avoid repelling other parents or causing other kids to feel devalued, though, heed the words "a little."

In their book *Loving Your Child Too Much*, Drs. Tim Clinton and Gary Sibcy share insight on how to make the most of public affirmation: "Make sure he hears you. Your son might act embarrassed when you boast about him, but inside he's beaming with joy."[10]

The camp we attend ends the closing night with a tradition that obliterates all memories of bug bites and fear of heights. Cabin groups of five dads and daughters (or sons) sit in a circle, and each man shares words of affirmation for each child present. Then the final comments for each daughter come from her own dad. A powerful moment takes place when each girl's father looks her in the eye and says in front of eight other people why he's proud of her, why he believes in her, and why he loves her. This moment has such rich potential that we dads often spend time during all three days leading up to this event mentally crafting our comments. When our turns come, we want to easily remember our words so our daughters will never forget what we have to say.

The simple challenge for us parents is to worry less about what other moms and dads think and more about what our child hears.

> Worry less about what other moms and dads think and more about what your child hears.

Ask "What do you think?" Kids spend their whole lives listening to their parents' opinions, choices, and directions. So imagine the confidence generated when mom or dad asks a child to weigh into a decision or discussion.

Paul, a parent at my church, describes how he brings this idea to life in a way that doesn't come naturally to him: he simply asks his daughters for their opinions. Not choices about what breakfast cereal to select or what movie to rent. Instead, on a regular basis, he seeks their input about some particularly vexing problem or situation that is on his mind (or might be on theirs).

"For example, I might ask them how I can better deal with my long commute each day," he says. "Or maybe how we could save up for something they want to buy. Or how, as a family, we might reach out to neighbors during the holidays."

In fact, this technique has become so successful that Paul and his wife have built it into their family's routine. Once a month they try to have a family meeting where they mention an area of life that merits discussion, maybe organizing schedules or future activities. "It's a great time to sit back and be amazed at how our girls come to life when given a chance to share their opinions and be heard," he says. "We can see it in their eyes; they feel valued and respected."

Words of Caution

The message "I believe in you" carries the potential for counterproductive application, so it's important that we spend a minute on what that could look like. Through aggressive zeal for their son or daughter to reach a notable accomplishment, parents can set unrealistic expectations for their kids, or thrust them into situations they clearly can't handle. I know parents who try to convince school administrators that their child will thrive in the program for gifted students, when test scores indicate otherwise. Sure, standardized evaluations make occasional mistakes. So do parental assessments.

Additionally, a child can perceive a parent's belief as conditional when it only comes on the heels of achievement. And keep in mind the advice we received before from Chick Moorman to avoid relying exclusively on evaluative praise: "Evaluative praise helps the person being praised to feel good *temporarily*." And what happens during an achievement dry spell? Parental belief in a child will seem to also evaporate.

Therefore, follow this guideline: Don't push your child to deliver reasons for you to believe in him or her. Instead, express your belief for your children now, just the way they are—void of pressure to perform well.

> Express your belief for your children now, just the way they are.

Children especially need our belief when they do not succeed. In her book, *The Price of Privilege: How Parental Pressure and Material Advantage Are Creating a Generation of Disconnected and Unhappy Kids*, psychologist Madeline Levine, PhD, says, "We all want our children to put their best foot forward.

But in childhood and adolescence, sometimes the best foot is the one that is stumbled on, providing an opportunity for the child to learn how to regain balance, and right himself."[11] Your child's stumbles, in other words, serve as ideal opportunities for you to express your belief in him or her. And your belief will act as much-needed and much-appreciated stability.

This may have been exactly what Fred Rogers had in mind when he said, "How I wish that all the children in this world could have at least one person who could embrace them and encourage them. I wish that all children could have somebody who would let them know that the outsides of people are insignificant compared with their insides: to show them that *no matter what*, they'll always have somebody who believes in them."[12]

And from the wishes of Fred Rogers, we can move to wisdom from the Bible. In the gospel of Matthew, God provides a powerful example of how to express belief in our children when, in the presence of all who witnessed Jesus' baptism in the Jordan River, he declared: "This is my Son, whom I love; with him I am well pleased" (Matthew 3:17).

In far less spectacular yet powerful ways, you too can share this life-giving message with a child. Whether beside a river, seated in a circle, or suspended in the trees — no matter where you and your child happen to be — you can say "I believe in you."

BIG QUESTION #1

"Is my child convinced that I truly believe in him/her?"

A child will more likely trust that God believes in her when she feels confident in your belief first.

"YOU CAN COUNT ON ME"

God has said, "Never will I leave you; never will I forsake you."
HEBREWS 13:5

Remember when Scott and I were up in the trees at camp, balancing ourselves across two telephone cables? Well, it didn't stop there. Despite our wobbly start, our success on the first segment of the course had filled us with confidence. Now we faced the challenge to walk across a single cable.

I led the way—slide left foot out, then slide the right, with hands clutching the safety rope overhead. Repeat. And repeat again. My dancerlike grace ended when Scott grabbed my belt and slid his feet left-then-right toward me. Every sudden movement swayed us back and forth. So we slowly shuffled in time with one another. Not bad—nearly choreographed.

Our rhythm ended, though, when I reached the end of the cable, pulled myself onto the wooden platform—and left Scott on the wire. Alone and scared. Both hands squeezing a safety rope.

What kind of dad, I wondered, *would leave his son out there by himself? Should I go back on the wire to rescue him?*

No way. I sat on the safety of a solid deck, where, with just a few more steps—or slides—he could join me. I reached out to pull him over. All he had to do was let go of the rope and take my hand. No problem.

Yes, problem. Scott said he would not let go of the rope. Actually, he insisted that he *could not* let go. "You need to, Buddy," I said. "You're so close, you can do it."

"That's easy for you to say," Scott shot back. "You already made it. I'm still out here, and I know I'm going to fall!"

I thought about reminding him that his safety harness would catch him if he tumbled, but realized that might scare him even more—either that or encourage him to willingly take a plunge. Neither option seemed good.

So I said, "If you fall, I'll jump. I won't let you fall alone." To show him I meant business, I took a chance and scooted halfway off the platform's edge.

The safety harness would hold me, right? Wait a minute. That meant the equipment would have to stop two hundred pounds (or so) hurtling toward the ground. I began to wonder about the sound made when a harness rips. Then I imagined the *pah-thump, pah-thump, pah-thumps* made by a rescue helicopter. Scott interrupted my terrifying daydream with a single word.

"Really?"

"Yep, if you fall we fall together—I promise. Do you want me to jump?" What was I saying? The *pah-thump, pah-thumps* returned—but faster. Or maybe that was my heartbeat.

His eyes locked on mine. He wanted to believe in me. Then, as fast as a blink, Scott let go of the rope, grabbed my hand, and jumped toward me. I pulled him onto the platform. His face beamed; I shouted with joy. And, yes, relief from avoiding the big jump. In that instant, we became closer. My son learned he could count on me either to get him onto the deck or join him in a fall. He trusted I'd be there no matter what.

The need for someone to count on seems obvious when a seven-year-old is suspended in the trees on a challenging ropes course. The truth is, though, that this same need exists for all kids as they navigate the jungles of everyday life. Kids long for someone to rely on, because life offers plenty of opportunities for disappointment.

Needing a Hand to Hold

Evidence of that disappointment exists all around us.

- According to U.S. census data, one in three kids lives in a home without one or both parents.[1]
- A Hofstra University study showed that 100 percent of kids hear hurtful names in school or the neighborhood.[2] That includes my kids—and yours.
- The National Mental Health Association estimates that depression affects as many as one in five teenagers and stands as the third-highest cause of death in adolescents.[3]
- In a recent survey, our children's ministry asked hundreds of elementary-aged kids to write down the most important question they face. Forty percent expressed confusion over acts of violence they see or experience. Another forty percent wondered about the unreliability of family, school, or friends.

More than we adults ever realize, children feel unsteady and desperately want to grab hold of a reliable hand. No matter the circumstances, you can inject confidence and stability into the youngsters in your life when they believe they can count on you.

Once while swimming in the ocean, a large wave knocked over my daughter, who was five years old at the time. The strong undertow held her underwater, dragged Erin toward shore, and then began to pull her out to sea. As she slid past me toward open water, I looked down and saw my little girls' eyes wide open looking back at me. I had the impression she was smiling. Adrenaline and instincts quickly engaged as I grabbed her tiny arm. I pulled her on my shoulder and in a shaky voice asked if she was okay. She said, and I will never forget these words, "I wasn't scared. I knew you were here."

When your child's life gets rough, will she have reason to feel unafraid because she knows she can count on you?

Words Defined

Kids handle tough situations better when they know that in good times and bad, they can count on a parent or other close adult. But count on them for what?

To care. Everyone is aware of the demands of taking care of a newborn. We also know that the intensity with which a parent cares for a child typically declines as the child becomes increasingly self-sufficient. In contrast, his or her need to be *cared about* remains at the same high level.

For example, even though a kid might require less and less hands-on help to get ready for school, parents will be wise to maintain active interest in what happens during and after school — the times kids will face their greatest number of adolescent challenges, problems, and pains. We parents know that our children must learn to face life's tests, but they need not learn those lessons in isolation.

"We may not be able to make their problems disappear, but even the promise of our presence and concern will help ease their pain," say psychologists Dr. Tim Clinton and Dr. Gary Sibcy in *Loving Your Child Too Much.*[4] This truth applies to parents as well as adults who work with kids at church or in other settings.

The amount of time that parents have to be present and interested in their kids' lives, however, provides them with a unique advantage over anyone else — but only when used deliberately. Scott Rubin, our church's junior high ministry director, frequently counsels parents on how to use that time to stay connected to their kids by actively showing concern for what's happening in their lives. "Even though your child might act like he doesn't want you to ask about his life, the opposite is true," Scott says. "Your kid needs to know someone, especially you, cares."

To be present. Possibly the most powerful way to show you care about a child, and to establish yourself as someone he or she can count on, is by being there. Yes, our busy personal and work lives often make this very difficult. Yet children notice, and thrive, when mom or dad shows up.

It's been thirty-five years, but I still remember how I felt when I spotted my dad at my weekday elementary basketball games. He had to leave work early to be there; in fact, he was one of few fathers in the stands. He didn't cheer real loudly; my mom took care of that. But his presence in the gym clearly announced his reliability and support.

So does help with homework, family dinners, and program-free weekend hours. Psychologist Madeline Levine says, "Our children

ɩ more from our ability to be 'present' than they do from being rushed off to one more activity. Try to slow down. It is almost always in quiet, unpressured moments that kids reach inside and expose the most delicate parts of their developing selves."[5]

To support. It took about a year of working, after I'd graduated from college ready to start a business career, to discover that life involves routine and repetition. Sales activity had seasonal predictability. The same reports were due at the same time each quarter. Some stuff changed, but the job essentially remained the same. This contrasted heavily with the previous two decades when I had learned new things every year, met new friends, found new ways to cause trouble, increased shoe sizes — constant change. While life can seem routine to adults, kids' worlds are filled with wild unpredictability.

And they long for someone to stand by them as a constant through all these changes.

My friend Len saw that his son Joey faced many new challenges when entering junior high school, with plenty more to come. So Len decided to write a poem that described the unwavering support Joey could expect from his dad — the kind of support every child longs to experience from his or her parent. Although Len may not qualify as a professional poet, in this case it served as the perfect vehicle to convey the words he wanted to share with his son.

Always in Your Corner

Regardless of the battle,
Be it big or small.
Regardless of the opponent you face,
Be it from within or from afar.
Regardless of your odds of winning,
Or the risk you run by fighting,

Neither time, nor size, nor difficulty,
Will ever change my stance.
My stance will always be with you,
By your side and stride for stride.
My stance will always be for you,
Regardless of the highs or the lows.
While we may not always see eye to eye,
Or agree on where you will land.
On this you can always and forever count on,
That it is in your corner that I will always stand.

To understand. A child frequently needs for a parent to set aside the temptation to instruct or give advice in favor of simply sharing in the moment at hand: a moment that offers a reason to cheer, to laugh, to cry—and always to listen. Your child will see these reactions as tangible expressions that she can count on you to understand the circumstances she is dealing with.

My daughter and I enjoy simple date nights that usually involve dessert. One evening we spent our first hour laughing and chatting over nothing important. She has a wit that always makes me chuckle. Then Erin began to describe a difficult situation she faced with a friend, and soon tears filled her eyes as she shared her hurt feelings with me. I count that second hour as one of the most important I ever spent with my daughter, even though I probably spoke fewer than a dozen words, none of which were instructional. More importantly, I looked her in the eye and kept waving off the waitress—Erin needed someone to listen, distraction-free. On our drive home she said, "Thanks for talking with me. I feel lots better now."

Sometimes the words kids really need to hear are those they say to a parent willing to listen.

At other times, it's important to know when to back away. For six years I coached my son's basketball teams, but that all changed when he made his school's seventh grade squad. The night before his first game, I announced the arrival of a new era. "I'm not your coach anymore; I'm now your biggest cheerleader." I remembered how great it felt to have a dad who cheered me on; now Scott knew that I understood what he did and did not need — and that I realized one coach is plenty.

To keep commitments. If you can agree to only one action item from this entire chapter, then I suggest you become great at keeping commitments to your child. Big or small. Short term or long term. Why? Because you can hit homeruns on the previous four points and still lose the game if you strike out on keeping your word.

> Become great at keeping commitments to your child.

In a survey completed by 175 fourth- and fifth-grade children in our church, only forty percent rated their parents' ability to keep commitments as "always." More sobering still is the fact that twenty-four percent rated parents "never" or "sometimes" able to keep a commitment.

This information illustrates a problem. Why? Because kids need the stability of believing they have parents they can rate "always" with respect to commitments. Even in a church, those parents seem to be tough to find.

We've all heard of the divorced dad whose kids watch the clock and fill with disappointment because he's late again — or the mom who frequently finds other priorities on "her" weekend with the children. But what about the homes with a parent more committed to the deal at work than dinner at home?

The *Wall Street Journal* reported that less than one in three kids eats an evening meal with both parents.[6] While you might feel tempted to think that the family dinner exists as an old-fashioned institution like sock hops and soda shops, consider this: the same *Journal* article cited statistics from the National Center on Addiction and Substance Abuse that teens from families that almost never eat dinner together are seventy-two percent more likely than an average teenager to use illegal drugs, cigarettes, and alcohol.

My mom was right: Never skip a meal. Funny, I thought that saying only applied to me as a kid.

To assure that your child would give you the highest rating, let's start with keeping commitments as the first of two practical strategies to help you communicate the message "You can count on me."

Words Put to Use — Two Decisions Anyone Can Make

Make Commitments and Keep Them

The formula for successfully keeping commitments to our kids is easy to state and sometimes hard to do: Make the tough choices. Marta, a coworker, describes the reality of what that has looked like in her family.

Over her twenty years as a mom, she's attended hundreds of activities involving her kids. With such an impressive track record, they learned long ago to count on Marta as a parent who shows up. But the road to that reputation has not always been smooth — or easy to stay on.

Recently, her son Jordan had a baseball tournament six hours away. On the same weekend, Marta had an opportunity to participate in a special church program she wrote that would be attended by nearly 15,000 people. In other words, a potential career highlight.

Likewise, six games in two days sounded like a highlight weekend to her fourteen-year old. Her decision, his activity or her own?

One night after dinner, Jordan told her, "Mom, if you want to stay home that weekend, you can. I know this is important to you."

Marta replied, "Yeah, Jordan, it is. But not as important as watching you play baseball."

A year later, Marta adds, "I'll always remember his smile that came from knowing I chose him."

In that critical moment with her son, this mom realized that the payoff from a well-earned record of commitments is that her son knows how important he is to her—not based solely on what she says, but also by what she chooses.

The choices a parent makes will either validate or undermine the message "You can count on me." In this example, Marta made a good choice in a tough situation. Granted, not all circumstances allow for such momentous decisions. Kids definitely must learn that all members of the family sacrifice for one another, not just mom and dad. And on more numerous occasions, parents face significantly smaller-scale decisions.

My wife, Becky, earns high marks in this area. She has never, to my knowledge, missed a time that she was supposed to show up for kids—ours or anyone else's. Not because she has abundant time. Between her work, active volunteer schedule, church, social circles, and keeping me in check, she's busy. Instead, she's very wise about what she'll commit to—and then makes those commitments her highest priority.

> The choices a parent makes will either validate or undermine the message "You can count on me."

We can all dramatically increase our reliability by making only those commitments we're determined to keep—and then making them our highest priority.

This principle also applies to adults who work with kids at church. If you're a Sunday school teacher or small group leader, you'll dramatically increase the impact you have on young lives when you consistently show up.

Thoughtfully agree to any role you take on; then prove to the little people looking up to you that they can count on you. The volunteers in our children's ministry who see the greatest amount of change in the kids they work with are the same volunteers who have the most consistent attendance patterns.

Typically when commitments are broken with kids, it's because a parent (or other important adult) allows life to reshuffle his or her priorities. I'm not saying to ignore your own life in order to serve your kids 24/7. What I am saying is that when you've committed to go someplace or do something with your kids, then don't let "something better" come along and change your plans.

It may hurt to see this in print, but your kids don't honestly understand when you fail to do what you promised. Sure, a son or daughter might act like it didn't matter when you weren't able to help with the homework project, even though you said you would. Don't kid yourself. He or she looked forward to your help, wondered when you would show up, and at some point resigned to the disappointing fact that you didn't. No excuse will erase that experience.

On the positive side of the coin, you'll delight kids when you demonstrate reliability. In addition, your example will help them develop their own commitment-keeping habits.

Partner with Kids in Activities

By playing, working, and learning with a child, you display genuine interest in him or her—a wonderful quality in you for kids to count on. In fact, we might have a few nearby experts on this topic who can teach us plenty.

Grandparents with close relationships to kids, church small group leaders who enjoy strong rapport with their teams, and that incredible

Girl Scout leader whom everyone loves all share a common secret ingredient: they don't merely watch fun happen, they enthusiastically engage in it. The lesson we can learn from them? Sometimes we need to create the activities, other times we simply need to jump into a child's world. Warning: effort required.

Want to build your relationship with a daughter? Play a game with her. If she's three, grab a doll, ask for her suggestions on how to play, and enter her pretend world. If she's thirteen, grab your tennis rackets and walk onto a court. Just make sure you resist the urge to coach her shots and turn your time into a lesson. In both situations, you'll send the message "You can count on me—for fun." And who knows when the lighthearted conversation might meander toward a heartfelt moment.

Greg, a dad at our church, took advantage of one such opportunity with his eleven-year old daughter, due to his willingness to invest enough time to let a conversation drift. "Megan and I enjoy paddling a canoe up and down the river," he explains. "On one of these recent trips, our conversation went deep, highlighted by my promise that I will always be there for her, even though I will give her more and more freedom as she matures."

Life includes much more than dolls, tennis games, and canoe adventures; so what about when the situations are anything but fun? My friend and mentor, Dick, decided to prepare for those moments by assuring his sons that they could rely on him and his wife, no matter the circumstances. "You'll face lots of decisions, and we will stand by your side when you make good choices—*and bad choices*," he told them.

Dick says, "Although for the most part they made good decisions, there were times they took us up on that offer. We would partner with them in feeling some of the consequences and prices to be paid. The proof was in our presence at those times—much more so than

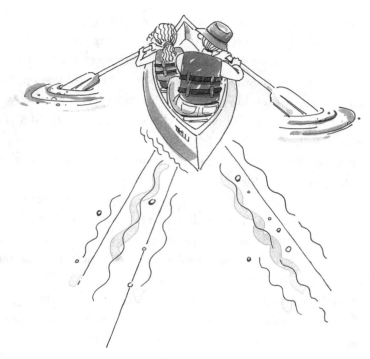

our words. But they learned they could count on us in good times and bad."

Yes, effective parenting requires a multitude of prices we must pay. Author and popular columnist Betsy Hart describes this necessary reality in *It Takes a Parent*: "We have to understand the cost. I don't mean the dollars-and-cents cost of raising our kids, or even hours on a clock. I mean the personal cost of investing in their lives."[7]

The commitment you make to actively participate in life with your kids may well end up as the best investment you ever make.

Words of Caution

The possibility exists, though, to overinvest in youngsters to the point of stifling their ability to grow and flourish. This typically occurs when moms and dads see their role as arranging a trouble-free life for a child. When this becomes a pattern, long-term damage can overshadow short-term serenity. Madeline Levine says, "Parents who persistently fall on the side of intervening for their child, as opposed to supporting their child's attempts to problem solve, interfere with the most important task of childhood and adolescence: the development of a sense of self."[8]

Reliable signs of excessive involvement are children who believe they don't need to follow other adults' rules, who show little concern about the consequences of their behavior, and who avoid looking for solutions to problems. Instead, they wait for mom or dad. A preliminary sign: no desire to pick up belongings or clean messes they caused. If you want to check on the reliability of these indicators, ask school teachers or children's ministry workers.

Children can also learn to rely on a parent's blatantly negative qualities — controlling, yelling, disappointing, embarrassing, the list could go on for pages. Challenge yourself by considering what your children can rely on you for right now — positive and negative. Of course no one's perfect. Yet while no one's keeping score on your parenting efforts, all those plusses and minuses will accumulate to equal some measure of reliability — good or not so good — according to your kids.

In our children's ministry, parents typically pick up their kids within fifteen minutes after the main church service ends. One Sunday morning, two children remained in our four-year-old area for an additional fifteen minutes after all the others had departed. As they played together to occupy time, one boy said to the other, "Is your mom a 'later tater' like my mom?"

Cute words? Sure. Yet also a clear sign that this child has learned to count on something negative about his mom. As this boy grows older, he might not remember the specific reasons why he believes this about her, but his belief will be strong and sure. What do you want your kids to believe about you?

My friend Dave wondered about that same question. "I tried asking both my daughters if there was ever a time that I told them I believed in them or that they could count on me," he said. "Neither one could remember anything in particular. That's okay, because what matters is helping them to achieve their own self confidence. When they believe in you and they know they can count on you, they will be able to do tremendous things."

Hold on to hope, though, that later on in life a son or daughter will remember you had a lot to do with the confidence they possess. On the eve of leaving for college, for instance, Jamie wrote a letter to her parents — a letter filled with words every parent longs to hear:

Dear Mom and Dad,

I sit here and try to put into words what is going through my head as I'm trying to say goodbye. How can I say goodbye to the two people who have stuck by my side no matter what in life,

I sit here and try to put into words what is going through my head as I'm trying to say goodbye. How can I say goodbye to the two people who have stuck by my side no matter what in life, who have loved me unconditionally through the good times and the bad?

I want to thank you guys for always supporting me, even when you didn't agree with me in the first place. I want to thank you for constantly building into me, even when I didn't want to hear what you had to say. I want to thank you for offering shoulders to cry on when you didn't even know what I was crying about. I want to thank you for praying for me each and every day, knowing that God would watch over me when you couldn't be there. I want to thank you for staying up until the wee hours of the night, just to listen to my heart. I want to thank you for laughter and all the good times we've shared. I want to thank you for constantly putting my life before your own.

Love always — your daughter,
Jamie

P.S. Don't worry, I will still come home and use your phone, do my laundry, eat your food, and ask for money — you're not rid of me yet!

Jamie's parents made a big difference in her life as a result of countless small decisions to stick by their daughter's side. Our Heavenly Father clearly articulates his commitment to stick with me and you too. We can look to his words as the greatest example of parental commitment: "God has said, 'Never will I leave you; never will I forsake you'" (Hebrews 13:5). His message to us: You can count on me.

Let's send that same message to our kids.

BIG QUESTION #2

"Does my child believe that he or she can count on me?"

When parental reliability exists, the leap to trusting God becomes an easier step for kids to make.

3

"I Treasure You"

Since you are precious and honored in my sight,
and because I love you.
ISAIAH 43:4

Martha Graham, who shaped modern dance in America, once said, "Dance is the hidden language of the soul."[1] Some parents watch their children at recitals and believe the language is very well hidden indeed. But not me. I readily admit that my heart leaps every time I watch my daughter perform. My pulse also quickens when I recall how close I came to making a huge blunder at her first dance recital.

Moms and daughters arrived early to allow plenty of time for the little dancers to dress, fix hair, and prepare for the show. At four years old, Erin loved all the fuss. An hour later, my son and I arrived early to secure good seats. As we turned into the parking lot, I noticed a dad walk from his car with a small bouquet of flowers. "Seems odd," I thought, "to give your wife flowers in public but, hey, some guys are more romantic than others." I even amused myself wondering what he had done so wrong to warrant such a splashy apology. My smile quickly disappeared when I spotted two other dads carrying fresh roses. That's when it hit me. Protocol calls for dancers to receive flowers from someone after a performance. And (oh no!) I'm that someone.

So Scott and I drove to a nearby grocery store and sprinted to the floral department. Spotting a colorful bouquet at a reasonable price, I grabbed it, and we headed for the checkout counter. As we stood in line to pay, Scott suggested I write something on the little card that accompanied the flowers, so I borrowed a pen and fretted over what to say — typical with rookie dance dads.

I took a deep breath and thought about how excited she felt, after months of practice, to finally have me watch her dance. So, with only a moment to come up with something, I wrote two simple sentences: "When I watch you dance, it's like you're up there dancing just for me. I love to watch every move you make."

My memory of her actual dance that day has faded, but I do remember that I loved it. And I also remember how she beamed when I handed her the flowers while my wife read the note to her. The power of that moment became obvious the morning of her next recital, six months later, when she asked me, "Are you going to give me another one of those notes?"

The bright pink, purple, and yellow of the bouquet paled in comparison to a black and white message that spoke to a deep, hidden language inside Erin. She felt treasured.

Feeling Special Matters

I didn't tell Erin she was nearly a Rockette. Nor did my note say anything about the quality of her moves — she was only four, after all — or that she danced better than anyone else. Instead, I communicated what I thought of her just as she was, regardless of accomplishment, acclaim, or applause. If she had tripped, it would have made no difference. My little girl was up there dancing, and for a moment, time stood still, and I saw nothing else. My note, hastily written, honestly communicated my heart. And it touched hers.

Words Defined

Kids long to feel special, the kind of feeling that comes straight from a parent's heart. Not as a result of performance. Not for physical appearance. Not earned at all. Children need to feel precious, prized, valued, or cherished—you pick the term—by mom or dad solely because they're kids and because kids are worth treasuring.

> Kids long to feel special.

To be treasured for no definable reason, though, might be a difficult concept for kids to understand. After all, their lives are constantly quantified by grades, athletic ability, percentile ranks, and a society sold out to the belief that beautiful means better. That's unfortunate, but it's reality. To combat this reality requires parents to reinforce the message "I treasure you" with two key techniques: deliberateness and repetition.

My friends Todd and Barb use generous portions of both ingredients to ensure their four kids grow up feeling treasured—as children of loving parents and as children of a loving God. The first Sunday of each month, their family gathers, lights a candle, and Todd blesses each of the children. One by one, each boy and girl hears life-giving words as dad gently cups their faces in his hands and looks deeply into their eyes.

"At times I speak to them about the meaning of their names and how I see that being lived out in their lives," says Todd. "Other times I focus on a character quality I have seen them demonstrate. Oftentimes, though, I simply breathe into them how precious they are to God and to Barb and me."

He ends each time with a biblical blessing: "The LORD bless you and keep you; the LORD make His face shine upon you and be gracious to you; the LORD turn his face toward you and give you peace" (Numbers 6:24–26).

Much More Than Congratulations

To deliberately attempt to convince a child that he or she is worth treasuring—independent of qualifications—can pose a steep challenge for parents. After all, parents are used to giving kids kudos because children often do exhibit good reasons for accolades. However, a world of difference exists between the messages "I congratulate you" and "I treasure you."

Congratulatory comments communicate support—good words to hear as long as they're not the only words. Parents who offer positive remarks solely for performance or appearance may unwittingly encourage a child to constantly compare himself to other kids. Why? Because he'll to know if he's done enough to earn notice—an unhealthy, self-centered perspective that considers all other people as potential competitors. A tough way to go through childhood, no doubt.

The treasure message, on the other hand, communicates a high sense of worth—and children who feel worthy are more likely to respect the worth of other people. Fred Rogers once said, "Every time we affirm how special our children are to us for being themselves, we're helping them grow into adults who rejoice in the diversity of the world's people."[2]

Parents can share the words "I treasure you" in countless ways and with consistent frequency because the message does not need to wait for new reasons. The only requirement is a parent with the resolve that it's the right thing to do, who then turns that decision into action. Let's examine several specific, proven examples.

Words Put to Use — Three Easy Strategies

Simplicity

When communicating with a child, remember this: the longer the message, the lower the comprehension. In addition, don't think for a minute your children will dismiss your words because they sound corny or trite. To a child, simple and heartfelt messages offered on an ongoing basis penetrate deeply and become part of an internal belief system.

Willow Creek's senior pastor, Bill Hybels, often shares a brief bedtime ritual he enjoyed when his children were young. He would ask his daughter, "If I could line up all the girls in the world and pick just one, do you know who I would pick?" Years of asking that question and telling her the obvious answer also included her responding "Me!" on her own. Bill describes the joy he felt one Fathers Day when he opened a hand-made card that began, "If I could line up all the dads in the world ..."[3] This example shows how a parent's words, spoken consistently over time, embedded themselves in a young girl's belief system so strongly that she, in turn, could share them with others.

Simple, empowering messages can arrive in other forms too. Jim and Sarah began to use what they call "pillow journals" with their three daughters ages eight through fourteen. "Sarah or I will write the girls a special message," says Jim. "The note can be short or long, but typically communicates encouragement, praise, or adoration."

Jim and Sarah delight each girl whenever they place a small journal next to her pillow, which she finds — to her surprise — either as she goes to bed or when she wakes up. The kids keep the pillow journals until they are ready to send a note back to Mom or Dad. Their letters can be anything they feel is on their heart at the time, questions, apologies, words of love, or thanks.

This process continues back and forth with each note dated and saved as part of the journal. Jim and Sarah hope each book will someday be completely filled with many heartfelt messages. "We want our girls to take their pillow journals when they leave home," says Jim, "to always remind them how much they are loved and cherished."

Bedtime conversations and heartfelt notes serve as great examples of high-impact moments. You can probably think of dozens of other affirming opportunities, many of which would require little effort. My daughter once brought just such an example to my attention — one I might easily have overlooked.

At least once a year, I ask her what I could do better as her dad. A risky question, but one that makes her feel valued. On one of these occasions, she asked if I wanted to know about something I was doing well. "Sure," I said.

"I like it when you call me Sweetie," she said.

"But I call you Sweetie all the time."

"I know. I like it and want you to keep doing it."

Like a 5:00 a.m. alarm, her words woke me to the reality that children can derive real pleasure out of a special, positive nickname. I've asked several kids whose parents regularly call them by upbeat, fun monikers what they think about this practice. Like Erin, all said it makes them feel special — which is kid-code for treasured.

Time and Attention

Renowned child development expert Dr. Benjamin Spock once said, "Perhaps a child who is fussed over gets a feeling of destiny, he thinks he is in the world for something important and it gives him drive and confidence."[4] Providing time and attention stand the test of time as two healthy, non-spoiling ways to fuss over a child—and to make him feel treasured.

For two years, I arranged my work schedule so I could volunteer as the art awareness teacher in my son and daughter's school. I don't possess a burning passion for art; in fact, I have the artistic touch of a bulldozer—meaning straight lines and not much else. And although I enjoy volunteering, that's also not the reason I spent an hour each month teaching kindergartners, first- and second-graders about different art forms. My ultimate motive was to make my children feel special. And it worked. They don't remember a single lesson I taught; neither do I. What they remember is that their dad took time off of work to help at their school. My memory has more to do with their bright eyes and big smiles for the entire sixty minutes of each visit.

Eventually their school hired a full-time art teacher. So I became a library aide. Different room; same smiles and same treasured feelings. Fortunately, I still recalled a few Dewey decimal system basics!

Grandparents, ministry workers, and family friends can easily join in the fuss-making. For example, my children love it when my parents or in-laws visit to watch Scott play football and Erin cheerlead. And it's not only relatives who can jump into this game: my son lit up recently when our junior high ministry director attended his basketball game—as did every other boy from our church, no matter which team he was on. If you are in ministry, check into schedules for sporting events, dance recitals, and other activities where a brief presence will make a big impression.

In addition to investing extra time with the kids in your life, consider how you will craft moments to give them special attention. As we've already mentioned, kids will provide plenty of reasons to celebrate successes. To ignore these opportunities would send a signal that you, as a parent, aren't paying attention to their lives — pretty much the anti-message to "I treasure you."

The challenge, then, becomes to show attention for accomplishments in a healthy, memorable manner. My friend and mentor Dick shared a simple idea that can make a profound impact on the way members of a family celebrate one another. He and his wife call it the victory candle — and the concept is simple enough for any family to use.

Soon after a specific and significant achievement by someone in the family, start a meal with a lit candle on the table. Turn off the lights, and by the glow of the victory candle raise your glasses of milk, water, iced tea, or whatever to toast the person and his or her feat. That person then enjoys the honor of blowing out the candle at the end of the meal. Record the event in a special victory candle journal. Over many years, entries could include awards won, first teeth lost, faith milestones reached, academic and sports achievements, acts of bravery (making it across a high ropes course, perhaps), and even workplace accomplishments.

By creating a standard ritual, everyone receives the same celebration. The result: the person feels personally celebrated—the accomplishment itself remains secondary. Long after the candle extinguishes, the victory candle's warm glow of attention continues. Dick remembers the sight of his son, twenty-something and on a visit home with his fiancée, sitting on a couch and excitedly reading each journal page with his wife-to-be, reliving the victory candle moments and memories. When done well, the "I am treasured" feeling transcends time.

While the victory candle burns bright for significant accomplishments, the need also exists to show deliberate interest toward kids' everyday lives. Fortunately, this is not a tough task. After I finish this paragraph, our family will gather for dinner. I don't know what's on the menu, but I do know at least one topic we'll discuss—we'll go around the table and give each person the chance to share his or her favorite part of the day. With the attention that one question brings, each person feels important.

Keep It Personal

Sure, a victory candle and mealtime conversations will provide public attention, but personal attention will supply even better support for your message. When you say "I treasure you" inside a moment that includes only you and your child, you eliminate much of the temptation for comparison with others. A parent who spends time to create personal, shared memories with a son or daughter communicates that child's worth. These moments need not be complicated or bursting with action. They take place when a parent develops a habit of spending hours—sometimes doing routine stuff, other times fun or crazy activities—with just one child and no one else. Just the two of you.

Sounds simple, right? But too many parents can't seem to figure it out. Unfortunately, when personal time and interaction don't take place, neither will opportunities to say the words kids need to hear. But when they do, the payoff can be grand.

That's what Mike found out from his twenty-year-old daughter, Katie. From her college, located several hours away, she wrote him a Valentines letter that described a few of her favorite memories:

> *I started thinking about when you were building the playhouse and you let me go in it before it was done, and mom was so mad. And then all the times we used to play baseball in the backyard with the blue bat ... I think something I miss the most is our date nights. I especially remember the ones we went to at church—the fifties theme and the beach party when my arm was broken.... If you go in my room after you read this, I still have the message in the bottle necklace hanging on the right side of my mirror. Go check.*
>
> *I want to say thanks for everything. I couldn't ask for a better dad. I've been thinking about you and miss you so much! I love you, Dad!*
> *Katie*
>
> *P. S. Don't forget when we fell off the wave runner and my swimsuit came off and I got a fat lip—that was classic!*

Katie feels treasured by a dad who spent time with her on countless occasions. As her words show, Mike proved her worth during construction projects, baseball games with a blue bat, beach parties, and fat lips. Just like the bottle necklace, kids will never let go of memories of their personal time with you.

If You've Multiplied, You Must Divide

Let's complicate this for a moment by adding in more children. Your challenge now becomes creating customized personal attention for each child—one size does not fit all. Common sense says that kids don't want hand-me-down memories, moments, or messages that they've seen used with other siblings. Yes, you need to spread your time out thinner so that everyone gets time with you. My son and I typically play sports together. My daughter and I do date nights, desserts, and bookstores. I go to camp with each of them every summer. My wife has her own sets of activities with both of them too.

With families that include several children, I've seen parents post activity schedules that carve out each kid's personal times with mom and dad. How do they fit it all in? They are willing, during this time in their children's lives, to spend less time involved in their own activities. They make it a priority to ensure they spend quality time with each child.

Sacrifice golf rounds? Yes.

Fewer nights out with friends? Uh-huh.

Decrease work hours? You bet.

Less time on the computer working on a book? Ouch—even that.

To parents who make these and other tough choices, the reason for their trade-off remains clear; they find great joy in time with their kids. Just like Mike.

The key word in that formula is "joy." Children will sense whether or not you really enjoy your time with them, both by the amount of time you spend and through the warmth that you convey when you're together. In *Loving Your Child Too Much*, authors Dr. Tim Clinton and Dr. Gary Sibcy describe how children will interpret such times: "Warmth is an emotional tone. You can hear it in someone's voice and see it in her facial expression and body language. It conveys the message, 'I like you.' 'I want to spend time with you.' 'I want to hear what you have to say,' and 'I value you.' You probably know people who lack warmth. Even if they don't mean to, they send the message, 'I don't like you,' or 'I don't have time for you.' "[5]

Warmth begins when you honestly want to spend time with your child. When that is the case, the temperature tends to take care of itself.

Words of Caution

As we know, too much of a good thing can be bad. Taken too far, treasuring a child can turn into worshipping a child. You can avoid this undesirable end when you steer clear of phrases that make unrealistic claims such as "the greatest . . . ," "best in the world at . . . ,"

> Kids will see through
> your exaggeration.

and similar statements. Sure, they might sound affirming. But kids see through the exaggeration — while other parents who overhear your praise fight a gag reflex.

So let's look for a healthy balance to treasure children without the worship. For instance, you speak honest and appropriate words when you tell your daughter that you would pick her over all the other girls in the world. That one's a keeper. On the other hand, "You're the best dancer in the world" qualifies as hollow worship, not confirmation of how precious she is to you. Therefore, toss that one.

I like Betsy Hart's advice in *It Takes a Parent* when she advises her readers to accept the fact that most children are wonderfully ordinary.[6] Plenty of opportunities exist to treasure ordinary kids.

Although it may go without saying, we need to say it anyway: you can make these treasured feelings quickly disappear with the wrong words. Derogatory comments, negative nicknames, critical comparisons to peers, belittling remarks — all these qualify as words kids should never hear.

We've all heard a parent make fun of his or her child in front of others and then respond to the child with the line, "Oh, you know I'm just kidding." Guess what? She doesn't know. And in those moments, she'll abandon any belief that her parent treasures her.

Humor, of course, serves a wonderful purpose in any family. Just make sure to include kids in the joy of laughter, instead of positioned as the punch line's sting.

Whether we like it or not, we parents sometimes need to speak strong words that coach, correct, or even discipline a child. Fear not, those words won't negate "I treasure you" messages (unless you overdo it). In fact, to truly love a child requires character building with words kids don't want to hear — balanced by those that grow their hearts.

In the book of Isaiah, God demonstrates this loving balance. In chapter 42 he describes displeasure with his people. He doesn't want his children to remain despondent, though, so he begins chapter 43 with a simple, clear transition toward reassurance: "But now ..." He goes on to express the extent to which he will care for his people, motivated by nothing other than their inherent worth: "Since you are precious and honored in my sight, and because I love you" (Isaiah 43:4). Much of chapter 43 expresses God's desire for his children to understand and take to heart a simple, yet profound message: I treasure you.

Let's follow his example.

BIG QUESTION #3

"Does my child feel treasured by me in a healthy way?"

An important consideration, because when a child feels cherished by a parent or other close adult, the leap to believing that he or she is a treasured child of God becomes much shorter.

"I'm Sorry, Please Forgive Me"

Confess your sins to each other.

JAMES 5:16

The clock ticked unusually fast—or so it seemed, which meant a meeting at work was chewing up more time than planned. Usually this wouldn't pose a problem, but the next item on my schedule quickly approached: drive my daughter and her friend home from morning kindergarten. Should I cut off the discussion or delay my carpool duty? It's only a three-minute drive, I reasoned. The talking continued.

I reached the school parking lot twenty-two minutes late. Fear gripped me when I could not see Erin at the pickup point. Panicked, I sprinted into the building. My blood pressure and adrenaline levels only subsided when I heard her say, "He's here."

Fortunately, my daughter's school prioritizes safety and doesn't allow kindergartners to stand outside for long. *Unfortunately*, they make kids wait for late parents in the school office, meaning I had to face the principal. After I signed the late-parent paperwork, red-faced and regretting my earlier decision, the incident officially ended.

Or did it?

I tried to talk around my tardiness as we walked to the car. "I drove so fast to get here," I said. My daughter remained silent.

Then, "I felt so scared when I didn't see you." More silence.

I tried once more, "I'm so glad you're okay." Still nothing.

Except for my nervous and meaningless chatter, the car remained completely quiet.

After we dropped off her friend, I made a final attempt to start conversation. "Erin, I had this important meeting that went real late. I just couldn't get out of it."

"Dad, you were *late*," she said with a curtness I'm certain comes from my wife's gene pool.

Still damp with perspiration from my parking lot dash, a somber realization washed over me. Her summary of the situation mattered more than my excuses. I broke the silence with a simple statement: "You're right — I'm sorry, please forgive me."

With an almost imperceptible smirk, Erin said, "Okay." And with that one word, the episode ended — from her perspective. But not from mine.

Erin taught me a valuable lesson that morning. Specifically, I learned the value of requesting forgiveness from my child. Not just offering a flippant "Sorry about that," but expressing an authentic apology. The impact from those words showed in her little grin, a brief display of what she likely thought (translated for us adults to understand): *Big Dad just apologized to a little kindergartner. Me, yeah, little me. It feels good when someone says, "I'm sorry."*

How Does It Feel?

In any kid's mind, such a conclusion will pay long-term dividends. Here's why: a child develops the ability to authentically apologize when she knows how it feels to receive an apology. The source of that logic: the Golden Rule. "Do to others what you would have them do to you" (Matthew 7:12). Substitute the word "apologize" for "do" and you'll understand.

The lesson learned here, of course, has to do with respect. Usually when the topic of respect comes up, the focus narrows on children showing respect for adults. And certainly our kids' display of respect for their elders stands solid as behavior we should expect; that's not up for debate. We need a wider discussion, though. Let's help children learn how appropriate respect feels and then trust that they'll, in turn, show the same to others. The late James Baldwin, author and social commentator, articulated the rationale for such faith when he wrote, "Children have never been very good at listening to their elders, but they have never failed to imitate them."[1]

If the message "I'm sorry, please forgive me" possesses such high value, then why do those words seem so tough for many parents to say? Child psychologist Chick Moorman explains, "Some parents worry that saying they're sorry and admitting they made a mistake will diminish their authority."[2]

> Why do the words "I'm sorry, please forgive me" seem so tough for parents to say?

Mom and Dad, the opposite is true. Moorman continues with her explanation. "Authentic authority flows from respect, and sincere apologies foster the connectedness and trust that is necessary for it to lovingly evolve."[3] Read that sentence again—maybe read it out loud, and then let that thought soak in for a moment. Can you imagine respecting someone unable to apologize? Neither can your kids.

Words Defined

Sincere apologies require effort, especially when you attach a request for forgiveness. You'll find that combination worth a try when you consider the result: over time, the apology and forgiveness process will become valuable and normal to a child. So stretch a little and just do it.

Do specifically what?

Show Humility

Fortunately, good coaching is available on this topic. In her book *Raising Respectful Children in a Disrespectful World*, Jill Rigby provides us parents with the first step for a sincere apology: "When you do make mistakes, ask your child's forgiveness. The level of respect your child has for you skyrockets when you're willing to humble yourself and ask for his forgiveness when you've been wrong. And following your example, your child will do the same for you."[4]

Did you catch the key starting point? Humility. Think it's a trivial point? Think again.

Dismiss the need for humility—the ability to acknowledge we made an error—and we'll diminish the impact of any attempts to apologize, because we'll likely do it only when cornered. In those situations, all sincerity in the words "I'm sorry" disappears because they're forced, not sincere. Eventually they'll slide completely out of our vocabularies. And at some point to come, count on our children to experience the same regression. That's a costly path to travel when being humble costs nothing.

A predictable price, though. Dr. Tim Clinton and Dr. Gary Sibcy offer a common sense explanation: "Children tend to treat people the way they are treated."[5] Seems like a human tendency to twist that Golden Rule into "Do unto others as has been done unto me." If you ever notice that some youngsters struggle more than others to apologize, keep this discussion in mind.

The humility we need comes from a simple truth—everyone messes up and has reasons to apologize. Even to kids. When you approach life convinced of your fallibility, a humble attitude will follow. Just don't get arrogant about it.

Make No Excuses

As a child, did you ever hear, "I don't want any excuses!" from mom or dad? I sure did. As a parent, have you ever said those words? I sure have. Do you ever offer justification instead of simply saying "I'm sorry, please forgive me?" Oh, I sure do! In a world that's supposedly adverse to excuses, they certainly seem plentiful.

Picture an excuse as a semi-trailer and an apology as a four-cylinder sedan. Hitch the trailer onto the car, rev the engine, shift to drive, and what happens? Nothing moves forward, for sure. The trailer robs the sedan's power, the tires squeal, and soon the sight and smell of burnt rubber fills the air.

In similar fashion, excuses weigh down apologies. Think about times when you hear people say "I'm sorry" but then justify what they've done. Politicians have made such spin an art form. But when we regular people try it, the picture it paints is rather unattractive — because it makes us sound like we're really not sorry at all. When we hear such explanations from someone else, we roll our eyes and think, "Whatever. You're blowing smoke. Let's just move on."

Nevertheless, kids learn they can avoid fault if they communicate enough extenuating circumstances. So the time has come to uninstall the hitch.

Before I expect my son to say "I'm sorry" with no rationalization, I must check to make sure my own apologies flow freely. Am I a "no excuse" parent with respect to my own actions? Are you? Remember that kids will treat others as they are treated.

In his book *10 Conversations to Have with Your Kids*, Shmuley Boteach describes a conversation with his children when he significantly ramped up his practice of no excuses: "There is no excuse, ever, for a parent to lose his temper, no excuse to raise one's voice. I realize that at such times I have failed you as a father, and I'm asking you to forgive me."[6] His sons and daughters will likely remember that moment for years.

In addition to remembering, they might even treat others in similar fashion. After all, the skill to apologize and request forgiveness typically comes handed down from a parent or other close adult who models such behavior. Will you accept this important role? Whether you're a mom or dad, grandma or grandpa, ministry worker or neighbor, let's look more closely at how to effectively communicate the message "I'm sorry, please forgive me."

Words Put to Use — Five Common Sense Lessons

For years, my friend Joe told me about his desire to be a dad who could freely admit failings and ask for forgiveness. Opportunity came for him at an inopportune time — an unusually rough morning as his third-grade daughter, Torri, prepared for school. Clothing indecisions, delays in loading her backpack, forgetting to brush teeth, all the normal morning challenges they faced every day frustrated Joe — and his mild manner disappeared. By the time he dropped her off at 8:25 a.m., Joe admits he felt angry and frustrated with her. For the first time he could ever remember, Torri left the car without sharing any conversation, prayer, or their usual hug. Not even a good-bye; just a slammed door.

As the morning wore on, Joe became increasingly aware that the real issue had been how he handled himself — that he had been impatient and unkind. Convicted that he must do something, Joe left work and drove back to the school. Once there, he asked the receptionist to page his daughter. A moment later, Torri arrived at the office.

Joe took her to a bench in the hallway for privacy. Once there, he clearly admitted his impatience and unkindness and how his words had been hurtful. Then he said, "I'm sorry that I was not acting like the dad Jesus wants me to be."

Torri's reaction to his apology caught Joe by surprise. A huge grin spread across her face. She threw her arms around his neck and blurted out, "This is so cool!"

"Confessing my faults and asking her forgiveness turned out to be one of those moments that will forever bind our hearts together," he says. Seven years later, they both still vividly remember that moment.

Three From Joe

Further examination of Joe's story reveals three lessons we can take away from what he did well. First, he apologized based on an authentic, heartfelt desire. Many parents, myself included, ignore such desires because we're so busy. If the thought "I should apologize" comes to mind, then act on it; that's your heart talking.

> If the thought "I should apologize" comes to mind, then act on it; that's your heart talking.

Second, Joe took timely action. To leave work and pull a student out of class might seem overzealous to some. But consider for a moment how much impact the same apology would have had eight hours later—after Torri spent her entire day in class followed by laughter and play with friends. An apology sometimes arrives too late to have full impact.

Third, Joe spoke clearly and concisely. With limited words, he admitted to impatience, unkindness, and hurtful talk. After the quick, poignant apology, he stopped—and worked hard to resist the urge to offer excuses. His decision to conclude at that point preserved the power of the moment.

Keep It Brief

Oh, how strong the temptation feels to continue speaking after the word "me" in "I'm sorry, please forgive me." But be warned: the potency of an apology diminishes with every syllable that follows. In fact, you can continue to speak so long that your daughter forgets you apologized at all. Keep it short, though, and she'll receive the full message. In fact, she might even think it's "so cool," just like Torri did.

Say It No Matter What

Sometimes our kids' immediate reactions to our shortcomings don't seem to require any apology. Consider these scenarios:

- Mom drops her son's mp3 player and now it doesn't work. Rather than offer an apology, she says that the case didn't fit well and that's what caused the gadget to fall. "It's okay," the son says, "I have all the songs saved on my computer so I can still listen to them."
- Dad promises to take his daughter out for a date night, but business conflicts happen two weeks in a row. He describes the big project at work and his responsibilities to lead a team. "That's okay," she says, "I needed to do homework anyhow."
- A Sunday school teacher travels all week and when the weekend arrives, forgets to pick up the happy birthday giant brownie she promised to bring for the twins in her class. With a sigh, she describes her hectic life. "That's okay," one girl says, "those brownies probably have lots of calories anyhow."

Even though a youngster rightfully feels let down by an adult in these situations, he might try to avoid dealing with that reaction. Disappointment with mom or dad is tough for a kid to handle. So instead, he downplays the offense's significance or develops his own excuses for the circumstances. So the awkwardness goes away, and the parent evades the need to apologize, right?

Wrong.

We can't—and shouldn't—escape the fact that in each case, these youngsters had legitimate reasons to feel let down. Contrary to some adults' fears, no permanent damage results from kids' occasional disappointments with the generation that precedes them. So let the honest feelings flourish—a process you can facilitate through an authentic, timely, concise apology such as, "No, it's not okay. I was wrong and I'm sorry—please forgive me."

Children who hear no such apologies—and instead learn to dismiss the legitimate liability of others—will eventually do the same for themselves. Play that chilling thought out further, and you'll see no-fault kids who grow into adults unable to take responsibility for their own actions. To combat this possibility, apologize early and often and to all to whom it's due.

> Contrary to some adults' fears, no permanent damage results from kids' occasional disappointments with the generation that precedes them.

Keep in mind that "all to whom it's due" includes other adults—kids constantly watch how parents interact with other grown-ups. My friend Dan recalled a time when his seven-year-old son, Bo, overheard an ugly telephone conversation between Dan and his brother. After the call ended he looked at Bo, and the bitterness he had felt a moment earlier melted into regret. Rather than attempt to explain the complex issues to his son, Dan developed a better plan. "I realized the damage I was causing," he said. "So I whisked Bo into the car and drove to my brother's house to apologize and ask for his forgiveness." Imagine the life-lesson Bo learned that evening.

In similar fashion, imagine the lasting impression made when a son sees his parent admit sins and seek God's forgiveness. We can all count on the fact that we will make mistakes. Our kids will too. How we handle ourselves after our errors forms lasting impressions in their young memories. Someday, they'll recall that picture when they consider whether or not they want to move closer to God—or to keep their distance. I want my kids to step closer to God. Hopefully you do, too. To that end, what example do we set?

Words of Caution

Throughout this chapter, we've focused on improving the skills adults need when they apologize to kids. But just one caveat: similar to the possibility of overtraining in athletics, parents can also overapologize to their children. This happens when you offer personal regret for experiences that are not yours to own.

For example, I've found myself trying to carry responsibility for traffic (I'm sorry that drive took so long), time (I'm sorry "Monday Night Football" stays on later than you can watch), and even temperature (I'm sorry it's too cold to swim). To express or imply personal responsibility in such circumstances undermines the impact of the words "I'm sorry."

While the examples I used might seem quite harmless, the problem occurs when overapologizing goes unchecked. When parents routinely apologize for a variety of life's challenges, the risk exists for kids to develop an unhealthy sense of self-pity or entitlement to a trouble-free existence.

To maintain a healthy apology lifestyle, consider this test: if the words "please forgive me" sound strange or inappropriate after you express that you're sorry for something, try a different approach. "What a bummer that it's too cold to swim" works just fine to communicate empathy or that you honestly share your child's disappointment. The clear action point here: keep the statement "I'm sorry, please forgive me" reserved for situations that require a personal apology. We both know we'll have plenty of opportunities to say those words!

Finally, make sure you also model forgiveness. Knowing that kids treat others as they are treated, a child's ability to forgive comes from the habits they witness. In the Bible, James articulates God's clear expectation in this area: "Confess your sins to each other" (James 5:16). But that represents only half the equation. The directive to confess comes with an expectation that when it happens, forgiveness will follow: "Be kind to one another, tenderhearted, forgiving one another, as God in Christ has forgiven you" (Ephesians 4:32 NASB).

The ability to confess (apologize) and forgive will serve as two important life skills you share with a child. The late Dr. Martin Luther King Jr. once described why that's important: "Parents need to give children opportunities to develop an ability to freely forgive. He who is devoid of the power to forgive is devoid of the power to love."[7] An important perspective when you consider the most valuable of all life skills:

A new commandment I give to you, that you love one another.
JESUS (JOHN 13:34)

BIG QUESTION #4

"How well do I model apologizing and forgiveness?"

When a child possesses healthy apology and forgiveness skills, he or she will be able to authentically approach God to confess sins and seek his forgiveness.

"Because"

*The reason my Father loves me is that I lay down my life—
only to take it up again.*

John 10:17

When my son was three years old, we spent six months in the
water together. Not constantly, of course, but for forty-five
minutes every Saturday morning in our local YMCA pool. We both
enjoyed splashing, playing games, and even singing songs as we held
onto one another during carefully crafted exercises to acclimate young
swimmers to water. When he turned four, we graduated.

Or rather, Scott advanced to the next level. I had fulfilled the
hands-on parental involvement, so my pool time came to an end. I
fought back the disappointment of my loss (ha ha!) and felt excited for
Scott's next swim class to start. When we arrived on that first morning, he felt something quite different—scared.

Scott had grown accustomed to having his dad in the water with
him. So much so, in fact, that he did not want to get into the pool
without me. Unfortunately, he hadn't realized he would be on his own
until we stood in the locker room, ready to enter the pool area. I knew
the instructor would begin promptly at 10 a.m., so I had one minute
to convince my little boy to face what to him seemed an impossible
challenge.

Tears welled up as he grabbed me around the knees. What should I do? Forcing him into the pool seemed like the wrong approach. Swimming in my jeans and sweatshirt also looked like a bad idea. Walking out and forfeiting the registration fee felt unthinkable. So I tried logic.

"Buddy," I said, "you're going to be all right."

"How do you know?" he sobbed. (Even a four-year-old can discern cheap words.) I needed a good reason — and I needed one fast.

"Because I'll watch you every minute through the window next to the pool."

"You will?"

"Every minute."

With that assurance, Scott agreed to try one lesson. As he walked through the door toward the pool, I sprinted out of the locker room to the lounge area, pulled up a chair next to the window and flashed him frequent thumbs-up signs for confidence. For the next three Saturdays, my little boy looked over at that big glass pane every five minutes to offer a smile and little wave. At week four the waves disappeared — he was too busy swimming.

Needed: Authenticity That Isn't Faked

While I'm sure William Shakespeare did not have our swimming pool challenge in mind, he nevertheless summed up the principle behind this little victory: "Strong reasons," he said, "make strong actions."[1] True, participation in a swim lesson might not qualify as "strong action" material. But it took all the courage my four-year-old could muster to walk alone through the door to the pool. It was not blind bravery, however. He had heard a strong reason to help him along: he would be all right because his dad had promised to watch.

Oftentimes, the difference between a boy or girl just hearing your voice and actually believing what you say depends on whether or not you provide an authentic rationale—the words you add after you say, "because." This word, used effectively as the start of a reasoned, rational statement, offers you a unique opportunity to make your messages powerful.

Today's culture often fails to include those valid reasons why. Watch a televised sporting event and you'll see many athletes claim greatness—even those players on a football team trailing by thirty points. Listen to contemporary music and you'll hear conceit woven throughout many young artists' lyrics. Read popular magazines and you'll lose count of the ads and articles designed to appeal to inflated egos. While team arrogance, teen vanity, and tease marketing won't completely undermine society any time soon, they do combine to create confusion. How can a child distinguish a parent's authentic affirmation, commitment, or affection from the hollow hype she hears virtually everywhere else?

> How can a child distinguish a parent's authentic affirmation, commitment, or affection from the hollow hype she hears virtually everywhere else?

It's time for we parents to take back authenticity—one "because" at a time.

Words Defined

As a parent, grandparent, ministry worker, or other adult determined to build into a child's heart, you almost certainly desire for him to hang on to your words with a grip that won't soon let go. The specific reasons you provide after you say "because" will act as handles for that very purpose. Skip the need to supply any rationale, however, and your words risk slipping into the background noise of his life.

Fortunately, anyone can increase the impact of what they say. You don't even need to turn up the volume. The fact is that children are more likely to believe what they hear when the words include justification. Consider the key messages covered in the first four chapters and the additional strength delivered from the words that follow "because":

I believe in you	*because* your generosity shows me God has given you a big heart for other people.
You can count on me	*because* you know I will always listen when you need me to.
I treasure you	*because* no matter what you do, you'll always be my girl.
I'm sorry, please forgive me	*because* I was wrong.

Words Put to Use — A Simple Way to Get Started

Too often I hear myself say the word "because" as a complete sentence, which only communicates "I'm in charge of you." Granted, some circumstances warrant a parent or other adult abruptly closing debate on a topic, especially when a child challenges authority or blatantly resists clear directives. The next chapter will focus on those very circumstances.

In those other moments, though — when we seek to build into a child's heart with a message he'll believe and remember — an explanation becomes vital. But not with just a quick "Because I say so." Rather, with a statement that answers the questions sure to go through his mind—questions that might include "Why is that true?" or "Why are you saying this to me?"

A man who attends our church sent a birthday letter to his nephew, Drew, to share wisdom valuable for a sixteen-year-old. As you read the letter below, observe how each piece of counsel begins with a truth and then includes an expanded reason. Also notice how the "because" message need not always include the word "because."

Drew,

At sixteen, life now becomes a game you play for real—what you do matters. So here are four pieces of wisdom I wish someone would have shared with me when I was sixteen:

1. Yielding to peer pressure never makes a person successful or popular—it always leaves you average or below.

Who wants to be average or below? I had the ability to lead, but didn't. I had star-athlete talent, but wasn't. I had the intellect for success, but wasted it. For too many years, I ignored how God wired me up in favor of trying to get people to like me. The result? Life felt out of control. Drew, don't give control of your life to other people.

2. Live life as though God is watching every second of it—after all, He is.

At any moment He can decide to provide incredible blessings in our lives, or He can choose to let life become real difficult. Sobering stuff, right? Fortunately, God loves you and me and wants us to be part of a grand story that He's writing—with a plot to have the whole world brought back to Him. Every word, every thought, every act from you and me either fits in that story or runs counter to it. And He sees them all. Drew, be part of the story.

3. When it seems hard or impossible to love your mom and dad, then fake it.

Those harsh feelings are temporary, so you'll avoid feeling guilty, silly, and childish later. I didn't believe my parents had my best interests in mind—I really thought they were clueless. I was wrong. The Bible says to honor your father and mother. So even if you have to pretend the love, that's more honoring than acting like a jerk. And I did the jerk-thing a lot. When all else fails, remember they own the cars and control the cash. Drew, in addition to your relationship with Christ, keep your relationship right with your parents.

4. Always smell good.
No explanation needed.
Once again, Happy Birthday!

Age plays a big role in determining how much explanation to use. A sixteen-year-old obviously requires more than someone who's only six. In similar fashion, words of wisdom will call for a longer "because" message than words of affirmation typically require.

Your Turn

Drew's uncle gave us an example in the wisdom category, so let's start with a shorter assignment: let's develop our own words in the affirmation category. The process is simple.

To start, write your child a note, email, or text message; feel free to use your technology of choice. Write "I believe in you because," and then list several phrases to finish that sentence, all composed of specific words you believe to be true. To authentically believe in someone means you have reasons.

Now read each statement aloud to make sure your words make sense—and that they sound believable to a kid. Keep in mind your child's age. Repeat this exercise with the messages that begin "You can count on me because…" and "I treasure you because …" Finally, move to "I'm sorry, please forgive me," but then only write the words "because I was wrong." (If this shortcut doesn't make sense to you, please reread Chapter 3.)

Keep Going

Now for the next step, give the note or notes to your son or daughter. If you have more than one, consider sharing one every Sunday night—a great way for your child to start the week. The words kids need to hear can also arrive as words they read. For a child too young to read, you'll need to adjust this exercise to include time for you to speak the

> The words kids need to hear can also arrive as words they read.

words you wrote. I suggest you start by saying, "I thought of you the other day, and here's what I wrote …" No matter the child's age, though, give him or her the note to keep.

But you're not done yet. One or two days after the note exercise, ask your child if she remembers why you affirmed her. Every few months, pose the question again. You need only a simple approach: "Do you know why I believe in you so much?"

As a weekly habit, challenge yourself to bring to mind how, and the reasons why, you've affirmed your child lately. Make sure this challenge includes the question "Have I shared the specifics with her?"

I tend to start such self-practices with good intentions, but then lose momentum. If you can relate to that challenge, then you may want to implement my decision to involve other people. Again, a simple task: ask your spouse or other close adult if he or she notices that you use specifics when affirming your child. Better yet, ask if they can recall examples.

Daily Use

Over time, your pattern of attaching reasons with your comments will turn the words kids need to hear into words that give them life. Michael Borba, author of *Parents Do Make a Difference*, provides clear examples of how this sounds in everyday conversations that any adult can have with a child:

- You are so graceful when you dance. Your hands and body move so smoothly to the music.
- You're very artistic; your drawings always have such great details and color combinations.
- You are so caring. I noticed how you stopped to ask that older woman if she needed help crossing the street.
- You always seem to have something upbeat and positive to say about people. It brightens everyone's day.[2]

After you become proficient with "because" messages in the words you say, try creative approaches with *how* you communicate.

As her girls grew up, my friend Barb periodically gave each of them simple-to-read books with key phrases underlined. The highlighted words reinforced how special each daughter was to Barb, unique ways Barb loved her, and the special nature with which God created her. Is this approach effective?

Barb knows it is. After several months of relational tension between her and one of her now college-aged daughters, Barb received the book *Guess How Much I Love You*[3] in the mail with these words penned on the cover:

> Just a reminder to show you that you mean the world to me. Even when I get mad. I don't know where I'd be without you! I love you!
>
> Love, Sunshine

An accurate indicator of whether or not your words make their way into the heart of a child happens when they share similar messages with others. Maybe even you.

Words of Caution

If, as you read this chapter, you realize that you need to improve your use of "because" messages, do so on a gradual basis to avoid overwhelming your child with a flood of them to make up for lost opportunities. One reason, maybe two, will get the job done. Wax on with multiple reasons and your young listener will begin to wonder what's wrong with you (or what new parenting book you just read).

Likewise, don't be concerned that you must continually come up with fresh "because" messages. Repetition is okay. In fact, you'll find that reinforcing positive characteristics in a child is nearly impossible *without* repetition. Reiterating a message typically wears down the adult first; kids rarely tire of hearing the same words that follow "because." Every night, when I tuck my ten-year-old daughter in her bed, I leave her room saying, "No matter what, you'll always be my girl. And that means I'll always love you." Sure, I could modify the message so it would sound fresh. But why would I? Those exact words, now a decade old, make her smile every time. I hope she believes them.

In a similar yet significantly more profound way, Jesus felt confident in—and could articulate conviction of—his father's love. One day Jesus told all those gathered around listening to him, "The reason my Father loves me is that I lay down my life—only to take it up again" (John 10:17).

Let's follow God's example and ensure that each of our children knows specific reasons for our love too.

Big Question #5

"Does my child take what I say to heart?"

A child accustomed to hearing "because" will possess curiosity about what drives God's love for us, and the Christian life overall, and be thrilled to see clear reasons exist for what we believe.

"No"

Now if you obey me fully and keep my covenant, then out
of all nations you will be my treasured possession.
EXODUS 19:5

In the game of baseball, a player's objective is clear: successfully run around all three bases and eventually score by reaching home plate. Along the way, he (or she) relies on the base coaches' instructions to remain focused on sprinting rather than on the other team's efforts to stop him. From the major leagues to Little League, the base coach/player relationship remains sacred; run fast and do what the coach says. Most base running errors occur when the player ignores directions.

But not always.

During a fifth- and sixth-grade league game, my son, Scott, reached first base on a short fly ball hit to center field. The team's power batter, Joey, stepped up to the plate. I knew my job as third-base coach — to direct Scott around the bases to score a much-needed run. With two outs, only two innings left, and the stands full of enthusiastic parents, pressure rose with every pitch Joey watched go by.

And then he swung. The ball went over the left outfielder's head. Scott began running the moment Joey's bat made contact, so he crossed second base in full stride. As he swiftly approached third, I yelled that the outfielder had the ball, but maybe he could make it home. But just as he stepped on third base, I saw the throw. It was good. Real good. "I don't think you can make it!" I shouted.

An unexpected comment for him at that moment, for sure.

Scott tried to stop, but slipped, fell to the ground, and landed ten feet past third base. "Get up! Get back!" I yelled.

He tried, but the throw came in and the third baseman tagged him out. Inning over.

As Scott stood up and wiped the dirt off his uniform, he shot a quick glare my way. I walked back to our bench with my head down to avoid eye contact with the head coach, the players, and the now-disgusted-with-the-coach parents.

After the game, I admitted my error to Scott. Unfortunately, I didn't stop there. I went on to explain that I had only told him "*maybe*," that the fielder had retrieved the ball quickly and made an unusually strong throw, and that I'd also told him I didn't *think* he could make it. (Yes, all blatant violations of the "no excuses" discussion in chapter 4!).

"Dad, you said a lot of things," he replied. "But you should have just said 'No.' "

Score one for Scott.

You Be the Coach

Maybe he would have made it safely home to score a run. Maybe it would have been a close play at the plate. We'll never know. What I *do* know is that he needed a definitive coach, not someone indecisive or overly permissive—which is, ironically, very similar to what kids need from parents and other close adults.

As Scott's dad, I'm definitely older and hopefully wiser than he. I hold a better vantage point to see what life will throw his way. After all, he's busy growing up—running the bases, if you will. Compared with any child, you too enjoy a broader perspective and deeper experience base from which to form decisions. The responsibility we possess to coach our children includes the mandate to say the word "no." Wishy-washy "maybe" or "I don't think so" statements won't suffice. Many situations call for us to speak that one, unambiguous word — "no."

Its meaning is clear. Its message is valuable. And oh, how kids need to hear it!

Author Betsy Hart explains why in her book *It Takes a Parent*: "Most of us want our children to be able to say no to all sorts of things someday — drugs, alcohol, sex, the influence of bad peers,

> The responsibility we possess to coach our children includes the mandate to say the word "no."

temptations that might draw them away from pursuing worthy goals and dreams, the wrong lifetime mate, even greed and laziness. But if we treat 'no' as something unworthy, how will our children ever learn to honor it themselves? How will they come to see it not as something ugly but as something that can be good and protective?"[1]

Words Defined

While the full value that Betsy describes will pay off "someday," children need to receive consistent deposits of definitive no's that start early and continue as long as they live at home. Just pay attention to how parents and kids interact and you'll see why this simple, straightforward word deserves significant attention.

Our church has a small indoor pond in an area where parents and children congregate after services. A two-foot wall around the water provides a great place to sit and talk — as well as a tempting place for kids to stand. Following one Saturday night service, a four-year-old girl stood on the wall and reached in to grab a coin someone had tossed into the water. Her dad, seated next to her, said, "No" and told her to get down. He then turned to people-watch the crowd walking past. She immediately reached in to grab another coin. Again, Dad told her to stop and turned away. The scene repeated two more times. Finally, after he looked away the fourth time, she swung her arm through the water, creating a big splash that soaked Dad's back. He spun around and gave her an angry look. With Dad's attention secured, she climbed down from the wall, put her hand in his, and they walked away.

Anyone watching this scene had little doubt who leads in that family—the girl. Even though Dad clearly directed her to stop, she knew compliance remained optional. The lesson we can learn at the wet dad's expense is that in addition to hearing you say no, a child must learn to take that word seriously enough to *obey* it.

> In addition to hearing you say no, a child must learn to take that word seriously enough to *obey* it.

Keep in mind the valuable benefit mentioned earlier: children who hear and obey "no" from parents will learn to resist their own urges and temptations. With that little two-letter word, moms and dads help children develop the internal strength to deny self in certain situations. Without it, they model "anything goes." Want to guess what time the little water princess likely goes to bed? Whenever she feels like it, I imagine. Or until the situation gets ugly, I fear. Now fast forward a dozen years and imagine her and Dad in a curfew conversation or boyfriend discussion. Will she demand that her testosterone-filled prom date respect the word "no" more than she respects it herself?

That thought hits me like cold water splashed on my back.

What about "Yes"?

To fully understand "no" requires us to look at its impact on a parent's "yes"—or, worded another way, a child's perceived need to seek permission. A kid's belief that he must receive "okays" from mom or dad hinges on his belief in the possibility they might deny his requests. If a child realizes that he will always, or eventually, get what he wants, why go through the formality to ask?

Maybe you've observed situations similar to one I witnessed not long ago. At six years old, Kevin knows how to get what he wants. His parents hosted two families for dinner — parents in the dining room, kids in the playroom. When Kevin saw his mom open a box of fancy chocolates for the adults to enjoy over coffee and conversation, he immediately left the playroom and its platter filled with cookies. Apparently, he prefered fine chocolate.

"No, Kevin, you have cookies," Mom said. He grabbed at the box, which she handed over to Dad.

"Sorry, but no," said Dad. Kevin, who seemed not to hear a word his parents spoke, continued to grab. So Dad covered the open box with both his hands. Kevin, unfazed by the situation, began to pry his dad's fingers up and bend them back. After a quick glance at the other adults, Dad felt embarrassed by the scene. He released his grip on the box. He didn't *completely* relinquish control; Kevin left the room with only one truffle when he had really wanted two.

To no one's surprise, this family's babysitter routinely finds Kevin playing with his mom and dad's belongings — believing permission is unneeded. Since he gets whatever he wants, why would he feel the need to ask? Do you want your kids playing with Kevin? Would you want your daughter to date him a few years from now?

Please don't dismiss Kevin's story as exaggeration. Or consider his attitude to be an isolated instance. He, and many other children, sorely need to consistently experience definitive "no's" in their lives. Then they'll understand the need for "yes."

The requirement for these contrasting words comes from a youngster's need to live within boundaries. (We adults know that a life void of limits will crash.) Any boundary rests its strength on the power to stand up to a challenge. Because of that, a parent's approval carries clout only when little listeners believe a real possibility exists to hear a denial. A lesson much finer than any fancy chocolates, for sure.

Now that we're clear about the need for "no," let's look at this important word in action.

Words Put to Use — Three Reasonable Responsibilities

Responsibility One: Be the Adult; Care Too Much

It's not much fun to deny, reject, or stop a child's action — and even less fun for him or her to receive that response. For that reason, "no" qualifies as a word kids *need* to hear but probably not one they ever *want* to hear. Regardless of the word's unpopularity, a young mom named Jenny knew that she must say it to maintain boundaries for her son, David, when peer pressure began to put a squeeze on him.

Third-grade David came home from school one day with a request: he wanted to see a new action movie that all his buddies had talked about during recess. Superheroes occupied much of his young imagination, and he spent hours reenacting their super-antics. No problem, Jenny thought, until she looked in the paper to check show times and saw the PG – 13 rating. David listened to his mom explain that some movies contain pictures and words inappropriate for kids his age — maybe even damaging. She said that if he still wanted to see the film when he turned thirteen, then he could. But for now, he could not go to this movie.

David skipped his snack and left the kitchen crying. He returned a short while later with a small suitcase that contained his action figure collection, one pair of underwear, and a toothbrush. He announced plans to run away.

At first, Jenny thought the situation was cute — but then she saw how mad and determined her son appeared. As she walked with him to the front door, she told him how much she loved him and that she didn't want to see him leave. Then she added, "But if you think there's a mom out there who will love you more and take better care of you, then I'll understand if you go." David paused with his hand on the front doorknob. Jenny held her breath as a single tear trickled down her cheek.

The logic of a third-grader may be hard to predict, but we can make a safe guess about the question that ran through David's mind: Does my mom take good care of me?

He stayed.

While a kid typically won't enjoy the limitations that come his way, their existence will help him feel secure. The reason: he knows that someone cares for him and stands committed to his well-being. Even though the nine-year-old would have struggled to put his thoughts into such words, David knew his mom actively looked out for him. To decline his request to see an inappropriate movie actually communicated, "I care too much to let you go."

Young David learned the location of a boundary that day. Yes, he tested it and other boundaries in the years that followed. All kids do. Why do kids (constantly!) seek to push against parents' limits? For one thing, that's a surefire way to capture their parents' attention. The girl who soaked her dad in the pond wanted to find a limit but found that none existed. She likely splashed him out of frustration — for what he wasn't providing.

In her book *Parent Talk*, psychologist Chick Moorman interprets the potentially elusive logic of youngsters. "Limit testing really means 'please show me there is someone in my life who will not cave in and surrender every time I create a test. Please be the adult, so I can relax with being a child.'"[2]

Responsibility Two: Be Willing to Do Something

Testing limits is a natural, normal part of growing up; ignoring a parent's clear, negative responses, though, can mean trouble. Children who willfully disregard a clear directive communicate, "I don't believe you really care about this, or me, enough to do anything about it." That's why consequences need to follow — with speed and certainty. Most, if not all, parents agree with the need for kids to pay a price for disobedience, which will vary by child and specific situation, a subject worthy of its own book.

Their concurrence at applying speed and certainty, though, seems to be a different story.

Moorman explains why swiftness, or the lack of it, has become an issue. "The average parent reminds a child nine times before taking action. When your action follows the ninth request, you teach the child that he can ignore the first eight." Jenny told David only once that he couldn't see the movie. Kevin the chocolate lover, on the other hand, repeatedly ignored his parents' refusals — and should have experienced consequences. The water splashing girl is a no-brainer.

Responsibility Three: Know How to Resist

As we parents consider our swift and certain responses, we need to use discernment about whether a child exhibits headstrong defiance or feels genuine dejection. The former calls for action; the latter necessitates empathy — without changing the answer.

My friends Abby and Neal knew how to stick with "no" and still exhibit compassion.

After house hunting for several winter months, the couple made an offer on a new home and put a For Sale sign in their front yard. One warm spring day, their son Tommy, a kindergartner, spent hours playing with friends outside. As he headed for home, he suspected that the sign in his yard meant he would soon leave those friends.

He ran up the driveway, crying hard as he opened the front door. Abby and Neal ran to meet him, looking him over to check for any obvious injury. Finding none, Abby asked what happened.

"I don't want to move and leave my friends," he whispered between sobs. "Can we please stay? Please?"

Both parents wrapped their arms around Tommy. "No, we can't stay. We're moving," Neal said gently. He and Abby repeated those words many times while they held their upset son.

> Consider how many decisions are made, or not made, because a parent fears a child's reaction.

In such cases, kids need parents who will empathize with how hard it can be to have your request denied.

But don't overempathize to the point that you don't speak the truth.

Abby and Neal could have chosen tranquility with their son. Responses such as "We'll talk about it" or "Don't you still want to move?" might have distracted Tommy and helped the young boy's tears subside. But would it have been helpful—or even honest—for Neal and Abby to disguise reality?

They stuck with the truth—something parents sometimes avoid for a very disconcerting reason: they're afraid their child will stop liking them.

Consider how many decisions are made, or not made, because a parent fears a child's reaction. Think of all the candy purchased in checkout lanes because moms don't want a scene — in which she might look like a bad mother to other adults or, oh my, to her child. Think of the junk food consumed (without parental objection) moments before, or in lieu of, a healthy meal. I know kids who have decided they will only eat a limited menu: chicken nuggets, macaroni, pizza, and sugar-loaded cereals. They typically don't load the microwave or pour the milk for themselves, so guess who has granted approval. Think of the inappropriate clothing purchased by kids (whoops, by parents *for* kids) as young now as elementary-aged. Go to a mall and visit a "cool" children's clothing store and you'll wonder; check out what kids wear walking around the mall and you'll panic. With your imagination now engaged, think of how many teenagers go out on dates with people who fall far short of their parents' better judgment.

Why does all this happen? Moms and dads want their kids to like them, so a definitive "no" disappears from their parental vocabularies. Nonparent adults often do the same. Sunday school teachers or youth ministry workers face a real temptation to tolerate otherwise inappropriate behavior in an effort to appear cool to their charges and thereby win acceptance — in the name of ministry, of course. Many grandparents do it in the name of love, but we'll extend them grace by focusing elsewhere. (You're welcome!) School teachers know they will quickly sink with a wishy-washy approach. So will Little League coaches, I've discovered.

The words adults need to hear on this topic are that kids will still like you even after you say "no." If your relationship with a child hinges on avoiding that word, you have deeper issues that need to be addressed.

A change in a child's respect for a directive to stop also might indicate an issue worth notice. When a son or daughter who typically obeys "no" begins to ignore this important word, parents need to probe for the reason. For those of us in ministry, a child's newfound lack of compliance with our restrictions often signals a problem to discuss with his or her parents. Sometimes the situation is as serious as a hidden trauma in a child's life; in other cases, it's as simple as a growth spurt or newly active hormones.

Words of Caution

It will be helpful to understand two additional aspects of the word "no." First, although underuse of this word causes problems, overuse will create its own undesirable consequences. You'll notice the signs of excessiveness when kids look for ways to avoid their parents. A daughter who believes "My dad never says 'yes' to anything" will eventually sidestep her father. A formula doesn't exist to determine the right mix of approvals and disapprovals, but authentic sensitivity to this issue should provide you with a starting point. If you question your own balance between the two, ask your spouse or other close adult. Or, if you dare, ask your child.

Overuse might also eliminate the possibility for respectful appeal, an exercise that can play a positive role in any adult-child relationship because it involves dialogue. Understanding how to reach a compromise is a valuable skill for a child to possess, because many issues in life require give-and-take. When a full or partial reversal occurs, a parent can bolster the learning experience with a short explanation along the lines of, "Now that you have shared that with me, I can see this differently." All requests for a parent to reconsider a decision must remain respectful, though, and not turn whiny or occur every time a parent denies a request or sets a limit. Healthy dialogue—yes. Heated debate—no.

> Understanding how to reach a compromise is a valuable skill for a child to possess.

The second caution centers on inconsistency. Some parents discover the need to say "no" only when their child publicly misbehaves. And while in those tense moments, the same parents often seem surprised that their child hasn't discovered the need to comply. A kid who gets away with anything she wants at home tends to believe the same parameters exist at church, the store, and any other public place. Grace, again, must be extended to extremely young children, as the skill of obedience arrives as a result of parent-child teamwork reinforced over time.

That time must start sometime, though, so why not right away? Betsy Hart explains the big picture at stake that drives the urgency: "If we do not train our children as youngsters to appropriately submit to our loving authority, if instead we train their hearts in rebellion, then how will they be able to one day submit to the authority of their heavenly father? Practically speaking, this means our children have to actually hear the word 'no.'"[3]

The inability to heed God's authority created problems for the first people—a trend that continues through today. Adam and Eve, although deceived, ignored the "no apples" command and took matters into their own hands. To ensure that others, including us, fully understand his expectation that we submit to his authority, God said, "Now therefore, if you obey my voice and keep my covenant, you shall be my treasured possession out of all the peoples" (Exodus 19:5). In this verse and many others, God shares the reason behind his insistence that we obey when he says "no"—he loves us too much to let us do whatever our impulses dictate.

It's up to us to love our kids in the very same way.

BIG QUESTION #6

Is my "no" respected and effective?

When a child can hear and obey "no" from mom and dad, she's likely to be able to do the same with God—who demonstrates his love by clearly articulating what we should not do.

"I Love You"
(Received and Believed)

*Children shouldn't have to look out for their parents;
parents look out for the children. I'd be most happy to empty
my pockets, even mortgage my life, for your good.*
2 Corinthians 12:14–15 MSG

More than a century ago, author Robert Louis Stevenson suggested an intriguing perspective on life. "Don't judge each day by the harvest you reap," he said, "but by the seeds you plant."[1] It was at father-daughter camp that I realized how relevant that advice could be to my own parenting in the twenty-first century.

Each summer, Erin and I spend three full days at camp, and I work hard to make every one of them count. I'm especially intentional when it comes to the late-morning hour set aside each day for one-on-one discussions. As veteran campers, we've developed our own ritual for that time—one that involves sitting on a small wooden deck nestled on a shady hill that overlooks a river. While we listen to tree leaves applaud in the breeze and watch squirrels scurry across the forest floor, we talk and munch on sunflower seeds. We even spit a few. Well, actually, we engage in high-spirited seed-spitting contests for distance, accuracy, and—my favorite—volume sprayed in a single spit. Sure, you may believe this sounds inappropriate for a young girl (or a grown man). So does my wife. But my daughter holds a different opinion—our time feels special to her.

A big part of that special feeling comes from a note I hide in the bag of sunflower seeds before each day begins. When we arrive at our perch, Erin reaches in the bag and—to her delight every time—finds her note. Each summer, the daily messages focus on a common theme. One year, for instance, the notes on all three days revolved around the promise, "No matter where you go or what you do, I'll always love you."

The last night of camp includes time for everyone to gather with their cabin mates and share special memories. Erin invariably highlights our seed sessions. I chuckle and picture how my wife would roll her eyes if she knew.

One morning after we had returned home last summer, I received fresh insight into how much our morning conversation times mean to Erin—and it has little to do with those seeds. This happened when I saw her looking at the notes from the sunflower seed bags—each one now secured in a binder she keeps in a secret hiding place for occasional reading. (Erin, I don't look. Honest!)

She's not hungry for seeds after all; she has an appetite to know that I love her.

While we dine on our sunflower seeds, those notes plant something important. Assuming Robert Louis Stevenson was right; the amount of love I plant into my daughter's heart is much more important than the love I might gather for myself.

Put in practical terms, my constant challenge is to determine whether or not I have sown any seeds of love with my kids by using words they hear, read, and best of all, believe.

No Assumptions, So Speak Up

We all know that love plays an important role in life. The Bible tells us that love bears all things, believes all things, hopes all things, and endures all things. We also can agree about the high value that comes from communicating love to another person—especially the love expressed by moms and dads to their children. But while all this love talk qualifies as common knowledge, too many parents fail to clearly and frequently tell their kids, "I love you."

In their book *The Blessing*, psychologists Gary Smalley and John Trent see the void around communicating love as a big problem—starting with the common rationale parents give for this misstep: "They know I love them and that they're special without my having to say it." Smalley and Trent's sharp reply to these parents is, "Really? We

> Love matters too much to leave it assumed and unsaid.

wish that explanation worked with many of the people we counsel. To them, their parents' silence has communicated something far different from love and acceptance."[2]

Love matters too much to leave it assumed and unsaid. That's the conviction of my friend Wally, whose commitment to express love has no boundaries.

A few years ago, Wally's friend Jeff fought and lost his battle with cancer. Before Jeff died, he talked to Wally about the intense sadness he felt for all the times he wouldn't get to spend with his eight-year-old son, Noah—heart-building talks, long walks, and many more moments that help a young boy on the road toward manhood. Wally pledged to help.

Wally, a father with his own boys, kept his promise by taking time off work to accompany Noah to father-son camp for two consecutive summers. During their time together, the two enjoyed adventurous activities, discussed this young boy's dreams and disappointments, and maintained Noah's memories of his dad. Wally describes the primary purpose of these trips by saying, "So Noah knows that his dad, and now another man, loves him."

Every kid — no matter what it takes — needs to know he's loved.

Words Defined

Love sits at the top of most parents' intentions. Many would rank it as their number-one objective. So other than reminding moms and dads to clearly articulate their love, are there any other challenges that apply to this topic? Yes. In fact, there's an even worthier aspiration that might take you by surprise.

A Higher Goal

I used to believe that, as a parent, the ultimate words I could hear from my children were "I love you." It's our culturally accepted way to express this deepest sentiment. It shows we have a healthy family built on solid relationships. It indicates our potential to bear all things, believe all things, hope all things, and endure all things. But while all those reasons are valid, a better phrase — a higher goal — exists. And that is for you to hear your child tell you "I believe you love me."

I didn't come up with this insight on my own. This perspective change arrived in a weekend message delivered by pastor and author John Ortberg. I heard what he shared more than five years ago, but it hit me in the chest and has stuck in my heart ever since. He said, "You're the parent — it's not your child's responsibility to make you feel loved."[3]

When I say "I love you" to one of my children and then pause expecting to hear that same phrase in response, unintentional coercion takes place. No, it's not wrong for my son or daughter to tell me "I love you." And the point is not that I should ramble on after expressing my love so that he or she can't respond. The problem rests with my *expectation* for a response—that little string attached to such great words kids need to hear.

Let me remain in confession mode for another moment—long enough to admit that I have sometimes used body language—certain facial expressions or a slight head tilt or even an upward voice inflection—to subtly beg for a response. I can almost make "I love you" sound like a question—as if to say "And do you love me back?" But while it feels wonderful when Scott or Erin express their love for me, it's unfair for me to fish for it.

The reason to use a blunt label like "unfair"? Simple. It runs counter to the type of love our children need to receive from us—unconditional love.

To fully understand this need, let's look at the basic characteristics of unconditional love. In their book *The Five Love Languages of Children*, Dr. Gary Chapman and Dr. Ross Campbell provide a clear definition: "We can best define unconditional love by showing what it does. Unconditional love shows love to a child *no matter what*. We love regardless of what the child looks like; regardless of her assets, liabilities, or handicaps; regardless of what we expect her to be; and, most difficult of all, regardless of how she acts."[4]

> Unconditional love is at work when a parent feels and communicates love for a child, even when that child expresses no love in return.

We can expand on Chapman and Campbell's definition. Unconditional love is at work when a parent feels and communicates love for a child, even when that child expresses no love in return. A youngster might not feel unconditionally loved if he believes he must say "I love you" in reply. Consider these potential questions that could race through a child's mind, worded in a way that we adults can understand:

> Mom, are you saying "I love you" because you mean it—even if I don't say it back?
>
> Dad, will you still love me if I disappoint you, even slightly, by not saying "I love you" when you say it to me?

Do children really think along these lines? Chapman and Campbell conclude that they probably do. "The sad truth is that few children feel unconditionally loved and cared for," they say. "And yet, it is also true that most parents deeply love their children. Why this terrible contradiction? The main reason is that few parents know how to transfer their heartfelt love to the hearts of their children."[5]

Anything that stands in the way of that message, including an expectation for reciprocation, must move aside. Because when a parent expresses unconditional love, the love transfer will feel complete. Completely great, that is, to both child and parent.

A Long-Term Message

As Terri Ann grew up, her parents rarely expressed the "I love you" message. In college, she began to notice how other parents clearly expressed love to their children, which created a desire in her to do the same whenever she had kids of her own.

Now that she does, Terri Ann says "I love you" more often than she can count, throughout the day, no matter the location or the situation. In a recent conversation, she expressed her love to her three-year-old daughter, whose response blew Terri Ann away. "You love me when I make good choices and when I make bad choices," her daughter said. "You love me all the time."

Those words fulfilled a mother's longtime wish—and achieved the higher goal that expresses "I believe you love me."

Words Put to Use—A Challenge and Three Tips

Bookstore shelves are filled with books that coach parents, grandparents, ministry workers, and family friends on effective methods to communicate love to kids. I've read several, and they helped me a lot. But despite all their more complex suggestions, I've found a couple approaches that have proved easy to memorize, deliver, and repeat often. "I love you, Scott" and "Erin, I love you" work well.

The Challenge

Before you assume I've grossly oversimplified this topic, let's look at what happens *after* saying these words, because simple phrases like these don't serve as end points that guarantee success; they represent the start of a challenge we all need to take.

Here's how it works. Say "I love you" to your child and then focus on how she reacts. Watch closely—her eyes will show if she believes you. If those eyes shine real bright back at you, all is well. If she can't look you in the eye, or turns away from you, then you have work ahead. Serious work.

Sound too simple? Just try it. Before you do, though, think of a time when you were in love, and remember how easily you maintained eye contact with your beloved. Sometimes for a ridiculous amount of time, I would imagine. Or think of the most recent moment when someone expressed his or her love to you. If you believed the person, did you look away? Of course not.

If your child's eyes sparkle back at you, then spend a few moments to develop a list of the ways you currently communicate your love. Do you say it clearly and frequently? Write notes? Give an unexpected gift with love as the reason? I know a mom who says "I love you" to her girls using sign language—face-to-face, across a room, or watching the school bus drive away. Whatever your methods, you've obviously tasted success—so your challenge is to determine how you will build upon whatever has worked so far.

In the event that no sparkle or eye contact happens, spend a few moments to critically ask yourself how you express love. Do you share words about your love or keep it a secret? Maybe your son doesn't receive the message often enough, so when he does, it makes him uncomfortable. Or consider what your child thinks based on your actions and attitudes. Do they support your spoken words or trump what you say?

Regardless of which situation you find yourself in, resolve to improve. A worthy resolution, for sure, but not a difficult one. Simply repeat the "I love you" then-watch-her-eyes process every day. Communicate the message in a variety of ways to creatively support your spoken words—such as notes, acts of love, a hug, holding a hand, or an occasional love gift. Just make sure you overtly share the message; leave nothing to assumption. This will happen when you commit to three basic practices.

Be Clear

Speak the words as though providing new information to a skeptic—albeit one who desperately wants to believe you. In his classic *Les Miserables*, Victor Hugo wrote, "The supreme happiness of life is the conviction we are loved."[6] You will convince through clarity.

Be Deliberate

Make declaring love to your child a normal part of your family's life, a habit that will permanently embed in a child's memory. National Hockey League great Don Edwards told a national cable television audience about the fondest memory of his dad: "One of the great legacies he left us, as well as countless friends and neighbors, was never failing to say 'I love you' each day to every member of his family."[7]

> Make declaring love to your child a normal part of your family's life.

Be Steadfast

You close this book and dedicate yourself to develop a new habit. You even begin to say "I love you" with new, unmistakable clarity. So now your son's eyes twinkle with joy and his young heart melts whenever you mention the "L" word, right? In case that doesn't happen immediately, commit to stay on a long-term journey.

Shmuley Boteach provides practical direction for such a journey in his book *10 Conversations You Need to Have With Your Children*. "I will keep telling them I love them, even if they think I'm being schmaltzy, because I do love them and I want them to know it always," he says.

"Still, kids are going to push you away, particularly as they get older. They are trying to cut the umbilical cord, trying to assert their independence, and that's fine, but you can't let it stop you. You have to remind your children, constantly and tirelessly, that you love them."[8]

Words of Caution

A possibility exists to misuse love's strength. Many parents are strongly tempted to use love as a leverage tool. I have done that myself. But instead of calling this act leverage, let's give it an even more honest label — manipulation.

For that reason, let's agree to never say words to this effect: "If you love me, then you'll ..." Even worse, we all know parents who send the message "I'll love you if you ..." While this can happen unintentionally, any characterization of love as conditional undermines all the positive practices we've covered so far. So when references to love happen, keep the unconditional quality intact. "I love you. That's not in question here. Now, I'm asking you to ..." Love as leverage is love lost.

Funny, with all its strength, love comes with no guarantees. So remain cautious with any expectations. This means that no matter how well you and I communicate, neither of us can force a child to feel loved. As author Bernard Malamud wrote, "Children were strangers you loved because you could love."[9] Therefore, we share our love with kids because we have love to share — and then we must trust that they feel it even when we don't know that for certain. Think of it as a one-way commitment, which is not a new concept by any means.

In a letter to the first century church in Corinth, Paul describes a model of a healthy parent-child relationship — one that resembles the love flow we've discussed: "Children shouldn't have to look out for their parents; parents look out for the children. I'd be most happy to empty my pockets, even mortgage my life, for your good" (2 Corinthians 12:14 – 15 MSG).

When parental love runs that deep, it comes from an authentic heart. An open heart that will express love frequently and passionately. A strong heart that is able to give without receiving. A faith-filled heart that trusts that the seeds of love planted now — one-sided if need be — will someday blossom more beautifully than anything ever hoped for or imagined.

Fred Rogers may have captured this hope best when he said, "Children who hear that they are loved in many different ways are likely to find their own ways to say it to the people they love — all through their lives."[10] Someday, they'll even say it to their parents, grandparents, and other adults who loved them most.

And, hopefully, one day to God — who loves them even more.

"God is love" (1 John 4:16).

Big Question #7

"Does my child believe I love him?"

This might be the most important question you face as a parent, because the answer will help a child begin to understand the concept of God's unconditional love.

A FINAL WORD

by Erin Staal, age ten
(with a little help from dad)

Life can be tough when you're a kid. Like if you get a bad grade on a test or have a mean substitute teacher. When there's a rainy day—because then you don't get any outside recess. Times when bullies pick on kids, or when fights happen. When teachers give you a ton of homework on a busy night—or on any night, I guess. When you go outside to play and nobody else is around to do anything with you. Or if you come home to an empty house. It's real tough when your parents go through a divorce, my friends tell me.

Kids *hear* some rough things too! Like mean comments about the clothes you wear—because they don't come from popular stores. Rude remarks because you look or sound different. Pressure for you to work faster from a teacher. Sometimes it's hard when the whole class laughs at someone who gives a really wrong answer—or when other dancers make a person feel bad about doing the wrong step. Nobody wants to feel stupid or clumsy. Do you? Some kids feel like their best isn't good enough—according to their parents. And there are times when parents have bad days and then lose patience with their kids. That never happens at my house (ha ha!).

All kids have their ups and downs. Some more than others. So why am I telling you all this?

Well, because I want to ask you a favor — please talk with your kids.

Maybe all the stuff that I described doesn't happen every day. But each day has its own challenges; that's for sure. So kids need a person who they can share anything that's on their minds with. They need to hear loving words so they don't believe all the rough stuff that they hear everywhere else. And *you* are the person who needs to tell them those words. If you're not that person, who is?

So talk with your kids. Tell them the words they need to hear.

Appendix 1:

DIG DEEPER WITH NEXT STEPS

The following questions and activities will help you put into practice several key concepts from each chapter. Although designed primarily as individual exercises, these materials also work well for adult small group discussions.

Chapter 1: "I Believe in You"

1. Write a list of several positive character traits you've seen your child display. Include a few words that describe the scenario that came to mind for each.
2. Ask at least one other adult who knows your child well to list positive character traits that he or she has seen your child display.
3. Select two traits that seem strongest in your child. Now write a sentence or two using words you can share with your child that express belief in her—based on each trait. Then determine at least one increased responsibility or privilege that you can offer your child that reinforces that character quality. Finally, determine a firm date on which you'll share all this with your child.
4. Does your child appear to lack confidence in any way that makes her avoid attempting new challenges? Determine one or two ways you will communicate belief in your child that build confidence without applying pressure.

Chapter 2: "You Can Count on Me"

1. List the various settings of your child's world: school, the neighborhood, extracurricular activities, family life, friends, church, and other major areas of life. Now, consider how your child might

experience unreliability related to the areas you listed. Do you and your child discuss the challenges he faces? Plan how you will start to talk about this topic in a way that won't feel like a pop quiz.

2. Write several reasons about how your child can count on you. Ask your child what she believes she can count on you for, and compare her answers to your list. Circle any reason on your list that she doesn't mention and spend time reflecting on how you will better communicate about that item.

3. What activity does your child enjoy that does not require friends? Commit to engage with him in that activity in the next two weeks or sooner. After your time together, ask him what activity he would like to do with you on a regular basis. Put that activity on your calendar and plan your time around it.

4. List any negative ways your child can count on you: short temper, yelling, anger, unreliability, constantly late, and other unfortunate attributes. Relax, though, because we all have them. How will you change?

Chapter 3: "I Treasure You"

1. Purchase a small spiral-bound notebook and a large candle. In the next month, begin a "victory candle" tradition in your home. Make sure to explain to your child what happens during this celebration. Also discuss how you will determine who receives future victory candle recognition.

2. With your spouse or another close adult who knows you and your child well, discuss specific and creative ways you can send the message "I treasure you."

3. Select one idea from number 2 and do it in the next seven days. Review the results with your spouse or other close adult. Repeat this process with a fresh approach for at least four weeks.

4. Bring to mind your child's friends. Who has the best relationship with her parents? Be brave and contact that parent, explain that you called because you've noticed his or her strong relationship, and ask for any ideas that parent can share.

Chapter 4: "I'm Sorry, Please Forgive Me"

1. Recall the last time you apologized to your child. How well did you do — was it brief and clear, or did you ramble and make excuses? If you can't remember one at all, then it's been too long.

2. For one full day, take a challenge to not offer any excuses. How does it feel?

3. List situations that cause you the most stress that involve your kids — getting ready in the mornings, after school, evening homework, extracurricular activities, report cards, confronting wrong behavior, even sticking to the word "no." Remember how you reacted in the most recent situation you listed. You now have a specific item to consider apologizing for.

4. Ask your child if he has suggestions for how you can do a better job apologizing (be age-sensitive when you ask). Then ask the same question to a few close friends. Do this on the day that you will not offer any excuses (see 2 above).

Chapter 5: "Because"

1. Using each character quality that you wrote down in the exercises for chapter 1, write a full description that follows this format (described in chapter 5): You are _____ (character quality) because _____.

2. Write similar statements (as in 1 above), but use character qualities that you would like to see someday in your child. Pray that these traits would be true for your child. Are they true for you?

Chapter 6: "No"

1. List the last three times that you yielded to your child after saying "no." Consider what you should have done differently.

2. Review these items with someone close to you, and ask that person to hold you accountable to say "no" and not change due to a child's pressure.

3. Does your child consistently obey "no"? If not, plan a specific moment to discuss this problem with him during a calm, issue-free time that's free of distractions and emotions. This discussion might require multiple installments.

4. Does your child consistently obey "no" from you out of fear? Now ask your spouse or other close adult the same question. Children should not live in fear of a parent. Discuss with another adult what might cause your child to fear you. Ask that person to hold you accountable to correcting this situation.

Chapter 7: "I Love You"

1. Begin today to say "I love you" to your child every day. To make this a habit, tape a note to your refrigerator that says the cue word "Love." If at the end of a day you realize you did not say these words to your child, then move on to number two.

2. Write a love note to your child at night and place it somewhere sure to be seen early the next morning. If your child is too young to read, write the note anyway and keep all your love notes in a special box to be read in the years to come. You can also purchase or make a small, inexpensive and unexpected gift for your child and attach a note that says only "Because I love you."

3. Take your child to breakfast or lunch on a weekend and listen 90 percent of your time together. Before your time is through, clearly express your love.

4. Let your children hear you say "I love you" to your spouse, your parents, or a close friend. When you consistently model the use of these three words, they'll become part of how your family functions — an extremely healthy part.

Appendix 2:

WHEN YOU'RE NOT THE PARENT

Whatever role you play, you can share the words a kid needs to hear even though you're not Mom or Dad. In this appendix, you'll find action steps that correspond with several "Words Put to Use" main ideas from each chapter. Of course these suggestions represent only a few of the many possibilities you can try, so use them to stimulate your thinking about how to become intentional as you share key messages with kids.

Chapter 1: "I Believe in You"

1. Whenever possible, watch the child in action to spot character traits worth noticing—with other kids, in a hobby or special interest, competing in a sport, or participating in an artistic event. Pay less attention to the results of the activity and focus more on how the child does as an individual. For example, if you attend a young boy's football game, then watch closely for signs of character that you can comment on afterwards. When you mention his willingness to hustle, strong will, team spirit, and respect for others, then he'll know you believe in him.

2. Kids love compliments from any adult. And the right words said to a child in a group setting work especially well. My friend Garry put this idea into practice when he attended Thanksgiving dinner with extended family. Before the meal, he tossed a ball with one of his young nephews. Later, at a table filled with relatives, Garry described to everyone how well the boy could throw. The lesson for our discussion: Offer specific, positive comments about a child when you're around other people.

Chapter 2: "You Can Count on Me"

1. You can make a big difference in a kid's life by consistently show-
    ing up. Susan, a ministry colleague, enjoys building into the lives
    of her nieces and nephews. So in her calendar, you'll find firm
    dates scheduled and special events planned months in advance
    with her young family members. They've grown to count on Aunt
    Susan for fun and for her to keep commitments. The action step
    we can glean from her: schedule regular time to be with a child
    who you want to build into, and treat your commitment as non-
    negotiable when other demands for your time appear.
2. Whether you're a favorite aunt, a family friend, or a fun youth
    leader at church, when you spend time with a child, make sure
    to focus attention and engage in activities that interest her. If you
    have a granddaughter who enjoys dancing, take her to the ballet
    every year. For a two-year-old who likes toy trucks, sit on the
    floor and play as long as he wants. Be sure to make truck engine
    sounds. And remember, from a very early age nearly every kid
    likes to go out for breakfast.

Chapter 3: "I Treasure You"

1. You can convey the "I treasure you" message with simple meth-
    ods that require little time, effort, or expense. My father-in-law
    has mastered this concept. For every sports season that my son
    competes in, he calls our home after every game and asks for an
    update. In a five-minute phone conversation with his grandson,
    he communicates how much he treasures Scott — a message that
    lasts a long time after they say goodbye. Notes, cards, emails, text
    messages — all are simple acts that can deliver profound impact.
2. You can make a youngster feel treasured when you visit routinely,
    especially when you show up for big events that center on the
    child like birthdays, dance recitals, and school plays. Always,

though, check with the child's parent first. Open communication with Mom or Dad will keep any suspicion from developing about your presence in their child's life.

Chapter 4: "I'm Sorry, Please Forgive Me"

1. Remain aware of the need to apologize to children. In fact, consider yourself a role model who demonstrates genuine humility and timely awareness of the need to say you're sorry—and the skill to do it clearly. When, as an adult who acts as an influencer on a child, you show that apologizing is normal, you'll help that child want to develop her own skills. Key to success in this area: apologize for little issues, because when you aren't a child's parent, a big issue may never develop.

2. Same goes for forgiveness.

Chapter 5: "Because"

1. Reread the letter to Drew in chapter 5. Consider sending this type of note tucked inside a birthday card each year. While the letter to Drew gives instructions on life, your note can focus more on affirming positive aspects of the child's character that you've observed over the past year. Include a challenge, as in the Drew letter, with older children.

2. Ask the parent for specific areas that he or she would like you to offer encouragement to the child. Imagine how much a kid will believe a message coming from a parent and another adult!

Chapter 6: "No"

1. Discuss with the child's parent what behavior boundaries to maintain with that child, and how Mom or Dad would like you to handle saying "no." Often, this requires you to be aware of the consequences the child regularly faces. You should also possess

a willingness to discuss a child's poor behavior with his parent. Keep in mind that while an adult who relaxes rules might make a kid happy in the short-term, you diminish the development of her sense of right and wrong and acceptable behavior when you tolerate actions that mom or dad wouldn't. Sorry, grandparents.

2. Again, make communication with a child's parents a priority. Ask if the child struggles with any disobedience and how you might help. A well-thought comment from you might help the young girl see the value of obeying Mom or Dad.

Chapter 7: "I Love You"

1. This message has great potential to sound awkward, forced, or strange. Make sure you have an appropriate relationship with any child before you say "I love you" on a regular basis, especially if no close family relationship exists. Grandmas, grandpas, aunts, and uncles — you're safe. Outside of close relatives, make sure you know a child's parents well first.

2. In all cases, though, you can demonstrate love through your actions. My wife and I enjoy a close friendship with Todd and Barb — a relationship now fifteen years strong. Possibly the most generous people we know, Todd and Barb flew my family to their home in Colorado one summer and let us borrow their recreational vehicle. Why? Because they love us. A wonderful vacation adventure, for sure. But also an incredible, memorable example to my children about how people can show love to one another.

Appendix 3:

WORDS KIDS NEED TO HEAR WORKSHOP

Workshop Goal

Introduce parents to the seven key messages from this book and help them begin to develop their own words for those messages.

Preparation Notes

1. Seat participants at round tables, which will support their ability to interact with one another during discussions and exercises.

2. Provide pens and paper at each table, plus an unlit candle (and matches if your facility allows them). Make this book available as a take-home resource that provides more examples and in-depth explanations.

3. To reinforce key messages, use a paper flip chart or computer-based graphics.

4. Plan the workshop to last either 90 or 120 minutes, depending on the length of personal stories.

Content Outline

Refer to the chapters in this book for examples, detailed comments, concept explanations, and key Bible verses.

I. Introduction

A. Introduce topic through a personal story that points toward the impact words can have on a child.

B. "Tonight we're going to concentrate on a critical area of parenting—words. Specifically, we're going to talk about how we can really build into our kids with the words we say."

C. Overview of workshop: Four short phrases, two simple words, and a fresh look at "I love you." Also, personal reflections, group discussions, and table exercises.

II. "I Believe in You" (write key phrases on flip chart)

A. Personal story (or use one from this book)

B. "What does Mom think of me?" or "What does Dad think of me?" can be one of the most persistent questions looming in young minds.

C. Parents successfully convey the message "I believe in you" when they practice two approaches:

1. Notice and name specific, positive character traits.

   Stop, look, listen.

   Ask others about the positives they notice in a child.

2. Demonstrate and articulate faith in the child.

   Adopt an attitude that expects the best in children.

   Encourage strengths rather than constantly correcting weaknesses.

   Develop trust by giving a child responsibilities.

   Express steadfast belief in a child in front of other people.

D. Personal Exercise. On paper, describe specific character qualities about each of your kids, including how they exhibit that quality. (Five minutes, then share with table group.)

E. Conclude this segment with The Big Question: "Is my child convinced that I truly believe in him/her?" A child will more likely trust that God believes in her when she feels confident in your belief first.

III. "You Can Count on Me"

A. Personal story

B. Kids will navigate life better when they know that no matter what's happening, they can count on Mom and Dad. Count on them for what?

> To care
>
> To be present
>
> To support
>
> To cheer, laugh, and cry when needed
>
> To keep commitments

C. Practical steps toward "You can count on me" include:

1. Partnering with kids in activities rather than always observing and correcting them.

2. Making commitments and keeping them. This serves as the proof of reliability, which children need and remember.

D. Personal Exercise. Write two things. First, think of the world of each of your kids. Think about school, the neighborhood, activities they're involved in, family life, friends, church and any other major corners of their lives. Then jot down your best guesses as to how they are experiencing unreliability. Second, write what words you can say that will express "You can count on me even if you can't rely on the rest of the world around you." (Five minutes, then share with table group.)

E. Conclude this segment with The Big Question: "Does my child believe that he or she can count on me?" When parental reliability exists, the leap to trusting God becomes an easier step for kids to make.

IV. "I Treasure You"

   A. Personal story

   B. Focus on a child's true worth—a child needs to feel treasured for no reason other than his or her relationship with the parent. Communicate this worth independent of qualifications—a real challenge because society places such high focus on external signs of success or beauty. The message "I treasure you" provides a healthy perspective for kids: they have worth without the need for comparison to others or any achievement standard.

   C. Keep the message simple, but repeat it frequently and in a variety of ways.

      1. Acts as simple as giving a child a special, positive nickname have an impact. Kids say it makes them feel special; that's code for treasured.

      2. An occasional written note speaks volumes to a child.

      3. Altering a work schedule to attend a child's activities or volunteer in school helps a child feel treasured.

   D. Table exercise—Victory Candle (refer to Chapter 3 for an explanation of this idea to use at home). "In a moment, I'd like the candle on each table to be lit. For the first few minutes, I'd like nothing but quiet. During that time, I'd like you to jot down on a card something you've done to build up your kids that worked well. This isn't about puffing up your ego, because everyone is going to share one success—so it's okay to do this. I don't know about you, but I'm always looking for new ideas from other parents. So for about three minutes, think of an idea to share. Then I'll tell you to start your victory candle time. Each person will take only about a minute or two and say your idea. Try to keep it at only a minute or two, and let's agree that it's okay to ask someone to cut it off if they go on too long or start preaching." (Three minutes on own, give cue, then fifteen minutes for discussions.)

Personal Exercise. Develop a list of at least three new ways you can communicate "I treasure you" to your kids. Be real specific and very realistic. I suggest you begin your list with "Victory Candle" or some other tradition.

E. Conclude this segment with The Big Question: "Does my child feel treasured by me in a healthy way?" This is an important consideration because when a child feels cherished by a parent or other close adult, the leap to believing that he or she is a treasured child of God becomes much shorter.

V. "I'm Sorry, Please Forgive Me"

A. Personal story

B. A sincere apology and a request for forgiveness show respect. Children who receive such a request understand that their feelings matter, that the apology/forgiveness practice is valuable, and that it's normal. Raise a child who possesses little or no desire to apologize and ask forgiveness, or who has no ability to receive an apology or dispense forgiveness, and troubled years ahead become easy to predict.

C. For maximum impact, humble yourself so you authentically say "I'm sorry, please forgive me" in a way that incorporates these five qualities:

Clearly

In a timely manner

Using the fewest words possible

From an authentic desire

In circumstances that truly warrant an apology

Parents find it tempting to continue speaking after the word "me" in "I'm sorry, please forgive me." With every syllable that follows, the power of the apology dilutes. The message then morphs into an explanation or excuse. Model "no-excuse" apologies. The lesson kids learn is that faults can be avoided if there are enough extenuating circumstances.

D. Personal Exercise. Spend three minutes reflecting on anything for which you need to apologize to your child. Write down any item that comes to mind, along with when you plan to offer your apology.

E. Conclude this segment with The Big Question: "How well do I model apologizing and forgiveness?" When a child possesses healthy apology and forgiveness skills, he or she will be able to authentically approach God to confess sins and seek his forgiveness.

VI. "Because"

A. Listen to these four statements and try to identify a common, key word:

1. I believe in you ... *because* the generosity you just demonstrated shows me God has given you a big heart for other people.

2. You can count on me ... *because* you know I will always listen when you need me to.

3. I cherish you ... *because* no matter what you do, you'll always be my child.

4. I'm sorry, please forgive me ... *because* I was wrong.

B. The word "because" makes words of hollow praise become solid. When you use the word "because," you actually are saying "here's why ...," and kids love to hear "why," don't they? So as you give your kids words they need to hear to build them up, make sure whatever you say includes the word "because."

C. Personal Exercise. Take the character quality about each of your kids that you wrote down in our first exercise and write a full description. It looks like this:

You are _____(character quality) because

_____.

Share this description over and over with your child.

D. Conclude this segment with The Big Question: "Does my child take what I say to heart?" A child accustomed to hearing "because" will possess curiosity about what drives God's love for us, and the Christian life overall, and be thrilled to see that clear reasons exist for what we believe.

VI. "No"

A. Personal story

B. Kids need parents who will establish firm boundaries. If this doesn't happen, children won't know how to manage themselves well. Children who hear and obey "no" from parents learn to say no to their own urges and temptations.

1. Parents help children develop either an internal strength about situations — or they model "anything goes."

2. The perceived need for permission from parents — their "yes" — depends on the perceived strength of their "no."

3. "Yes" has more impact when kids believe a real possibility exists to hear "no."

C. Children feel a sense of security when they hear "no."

1. Children know someone watches over them, cares for them, and stands committed to their safety.

2. Kids seek to find the limit, not the trouble. Why seek the limit? Because that's where the parent can be found.

3. A child who ignores "no" communicates, "I don't believe you really care."

D. Many parents shy away from definitively saying no because they fear a child will stop liking them.

E. Conclude this segment with The Big Question: "Is my 'no' respected and effective?" When a child can hear and obey "no" from Mom and Dad, she's likely to be able to do the same with God—who demonstrates his love by clearly articulating what we should not do.

VII. "I Love You"

A. What could possibly be said new about this statement?

B. A higher goal for parents. Are there any better words for parents to hear than "I love you"? Yes—when a child says, "I believe you love me."

    1. A child does not have the responsibility to make a parent feel loved.

    2. When a parent says "I love you" and then pauses (in the expectation of hearing "I love you" back), unintentional manipulation takes place—the child is effectively coerced into responding.

    3. It's not wrong for a child to express his or her love for a parent; but it is wrong for the parent to go fishing for it.

C. At-home Personal Exercise. Before the end of this day, look your child in the eye and say, "I love you."

    1. Keep looking—you'll know by his eyes if he believes you. If those eyes shine real bright back at you, all is well. If he can't look at you and/or turns away, then you now have a new highest priority—communicate love to your child in a way he understands and believes.

    2. Repeat this process every day in a variety of ways. Be deliberate—make this a habit that turns into a normal

part of life for you and your child. And be clear—speak the words as if providing new information to a skeptic.

D. Conclude this segment with The Big Question: "Does my child believe I love him?" This might be the most important question you face as a parent, because the answer will help a child begin to understand the concept of God's unconditional love.

VIII. Conclusion

A. Review by restating the seven key messages.

B. Issue a final challenge to put the concepts learned into use with children.

C. Consider reading the "Final Word" section of this book as an encouragement from a ten-year-old girl.

ACKNOWLEDGMENTS

Becky—Thanks for your love, encouragement, and all the time you put into listening and discussing ideas for this book—and for not laughing too hard at the odd ones.

Scott—Thanks for your permission to tell stories of our adventures together. The love and close relationship we share fill me with joy every day.

Erin—Thanks for putting your writing talent to work with this book and for allowing me to tell stories about some of our interesting moments. I'll always love you, partner!

Judy—Thanks for the hours and hours of work and wisdom. Your cheers, corrections, and graceful coaching built every page.

Paul, Bob, Mark, and the Zondervan team—Thanks for another opportunity to work with all of you; I feel privileged to partner with you.

Teri—Thanks for all the research, stories, and frequent counseling sessions—and for doing ministry together all these years.

Tim and Len—Thanks for building a life-changing ministry and for tapping me on the shoulder to write a book.

Christine—Thanks for your guidance and for reminding me that I'm not crazy.

Dick Towner—Thanks for every minute of every lunch and for your generosity to share wisdom with me. You make me want to be a better dad, husband, and Christ-follower.

Todd—Thanks for ignoring the miles that separate us so we can continue the incredible relationship we enjoy. You model well the role of spiritually leading a family.

Garry—Thanks for your steadfast friendship and for the hours you endure listening to me.

Brian and Dave—Thanks for all the years we spent around the breakfast table sharing life and the "number one special."

Promiseland Ministry—Thanks for radically loving kids. I love you all and the continual string of new days we discover together.

Bill, Gene, and Jon—Thanks for the opportunity to lead, create, and write—and for your patience with me.

Dad and Mom—Thanks for always believing the best about me, even when that meant stretching your love a little. Or a lot.

Becky—Thanks for constantly sharing the words I need to hear: "I love you." You receive two acknowledgments because I want to make sure you know how deeply I love you. I'm your man.

ENDNOTES

Introduction

1. Morten Christiansen, quoted in *Cornell Chronicle 2005, www. news.cornell.edu/ Chronicle/05/2.24.05/Lingua.html*

Chapter 1

1. Anne Schraff, *Wilma Rudolph* (Berkeley Heights, N.J.: Enslow, 2004), 13.
2. John Eldridge, *Wild at Heart* (Nashville: Nelson, 2001), 57.
3. Mike Kryzyzewski, *Beyond Basketball: Coach K's Key Words for Success* (New York: Warner Business, 2006), 14.
4. Chick Moorman, *Parent Talk: How to Talk to Your Child in a Language That Builds Self-Esteem and Encourages Responsibility* (New York: Simon & Schuster, 1998), 120–121.
5. Fred Rogers, *Many Ways to Say I Love You: Wisdom for Parents and Children from Mister Rogers* (New York: Family Communications, 2006), 13.
6. Michael Borba, *Parents Do Make a Difference: How to Raise Kids with Solid Character, Strong Minds, and Caring Hearts* (San Francisco: Jossey-Bass, 1999), 26.
7. Marcus Buckingham, *The One Thing You Need to Know* (New York: Free Press, 2005).
8. Rosamond Stone Zander and Benjamin Zander, *The Art of Possibility* (Boston: Harvard Business School, 2000), 26–27.
9. Josie Bissett, *Making Memories: A Parent's Guide to Making Childhood Memories that Last a Lifetime* (Lynnwood, Wash.: Compendium, 2003), 65.
10. Tim Clinton and Gary Sibcy, *Loving Your Child Too Much* (Franklin, Tenn.: Integrity, 2006), 113.

11. Madeline Levine, *The Price of Privilege: How Parental Pressure and Material Advantage Are Creating a Generation of Disconnected and Unhappy Kids* (New York: HarperCollins, 2006), 9.
12. Rogers, *Many Ways to Say I Love You,* 176.

Chapter 2

1. U.S. Bureau of the Census, Current Population Survey—Families and Living Arrangements, Historical Tables, 2001, *www.census.gov/population/www/socdeom/hh-fam.html#history.*
2. Betsy Taylor, *What Kids Really Want That Money Can't Buy* (New York: Warner, 2003), 134.
3. Stephanie Fosnight, "A Beacon of Hope," *Pioneer Press* (July 8, 2005), *www.pioneerlocal.com.*
4. Clinton and Sibcy, *Loving Your Child Too Much,* 145.
5. Levine, *The Price of Privilege,* 31.
6. Cameron Stracher, "Much Depends on Dinner," *Wall Street Journal* (August 8, 2005), *www.opinionjournal.com.*
7. Betsy Hart, *It Takes a Parent* (New York: Berkley/Penguin, 2005), 55.
8. Levine, *The Price of Privilege,* 8.

Chapter 3

1. Martha Graham, "Martha Graham Reflects on Her Art and a Life in Dance," *The New York Times* (1985), *http://www.nytimes.com/library/arts/033185graham.html.*
2. Rogers, *Many Ways to Say I Love You,* 140.
3. Bill Hybels, Weekend Message: "DadFest '06" (South Barrington, Ill.: Willow Creek Community Church, 2006).
4. Dr. Benjamin Spock, *New York Sunday News* (May 11, 1958), as cited in *The International Thesaurus of Quotations* (New York: HarperCollins, 1996), 86.
5. Clinton and Sibcy, *Loving Your Child Too Much,* 78.
6. Hart, *It Takes a Parent,* 81.

Chapter 4

1. James Baldwin, *Baldwin: Collected Essays,* ed. Toni Morrison, (New York: Library of America, 1998), 173.
2. Moorman, *Parent Talk*, 170.
3. Ibid.
4. Jill Rigby, *Raising Respectful Children in a Disrespectful World* (New York: Howard, 2006), 114.
5. Clinton and Sibcy, *Loving Your Child Too Much*, 78.
6. Shmuley Boteach, *10 Conversations You Need to Have With Your Children* (New York: HarperCollins, 2006), 130.
7. Coretta Scott King, *The Words of Martin Luther King, Jr.* (New York: New Market, 1983), 23.

Chapter 5

1. William Shakespeare, *King John* (New York: Penguin, 1974), act 3, scene 4, 60.
2. Borba, *Parents Do Make a Difference*, 41–44.
3. Sam McBratney, *Guess How Much I Love You* (Cambridge, Mass.: Candlewick, 1996).

Chapter 6

1. Hart, *It Takes a Parent*, 134.
2. Moorman, *Parent Talk*, 56.
3. Ibid.
4. Betsy Hart, Children's Ministry Conference, "Connecting With Purpose" Session 6 (South Barrington, Ill.: Willow Creek Community Church, 2007).

Chapter 7

1. Cindy Crosby, *Today's Christian Woman*, 27:5 (Sept./Oct. 2005), 28.
2. Gary Smalley and John Trent, *The Blessing* (Nashville: Nelson, 1986), 58.

3. John Ortberg, Weekend Message, "Parents and Kids, Same Planet/Different Worlds" (South Barrington, Ill.: Willow Creek Community Church, 2003).

4. Gary Chapman and Ross Campbell, *The Five Love Languages of Children* (Chicago: Northfield, 2005), 20.

5. Ibid, 26.

6. Victor Hugo, *Les Miserables* (New York: Penguin, 1987), 167.

7. Larry King, *My Dad and Me* (New York: Crown, 2006), 96.

8. Boteach, *10 Conversations*, 156.

9. Bernard Malamud, *Dubin's Lives* (New York: Farrar, Straus and Giroux, 1977), 248.

10. Rogers, *Many Ways to Say I Love You*, 95.

Willow Creek Association
Vision, Training, Resources for Prevailing Churches

This resource was created to serve you and to help you build a local church that prevails. It is just one of many ministry tools that are part of the Willow Creek Resources® line, published by the Willow Creek Association together with Zondervan.

The Willow Creek Association (WCA) was created in 1992 to serve a rapidly growing number of churches from across the denominational spectrum that are committed to helping unchurched people become fully devoted followers of Christ. Membership in the WCA now numbers over 12,000 Member Churches worldwide from more than ninety denominations.

The Willow Creek Association links like-minded Christian leaders with each other and with strategic vision, training, and resources in order to help them build prevailing churches designed to reach their redemptive potential. Here are some of the ways the WCA does that.

- **The Leadership Summit**—a once a year, two-and-a-half-day conference to envision and equip Christians with leadership gifts and responsibilities. Presented live at Willow Creek as well as via satellite broadcast to over 130 locations across North America, this event is designed to increase the leadership effectiveness of pastors, ministry staff, volunteer church leaders, and Christians in the marketplace.

- **Ministry-Specific Conferences**—throughout each year the WCA hosts a variety of conferences and training events—both at Willow Creek's main campus and offsite, across the U.S., and around the world—targeting church leaders and volunteers in ministry-specific areas such as: small groups, preaching and teaching, the arts, children, students, volunteers, stewardship, etc.

- **Willow Creek Resources®**—provides churches with trusted and field-tested ministry resources in such areas as leadership, evangelism, spiritual formation, spiritual gifts, small groups, stewardship, student ministry, children's ministry, the use of the arts-drama, media, contemporary music—and more.

- **WCA Member Benefits**—includes substantial discounts to WCA training events, a 20 percent discount on all Willow Creek Resources®, *Defining Moments* monthly audio journal for leaders, quarterly *Willow* magazine, access to a Members-Only section on WillowNet, monthly communications, and more. Member Churches also receive special discounts and premier services through WCA's growing number of ministry partners—Select Service Providers—and save an average of $500 annually depending on the level of engagement.

For specific information about WCA conferences, resources, membership, and other ministry services contact:

Willow Creek Association
P.O. Box 3188, Barrington, IL 60011-3188
Phone: 847-570-9812, Fax: 847-765-5046
www.willowcreek.com

Making Your Children's Ministry the Best Hour of Every Kid's Week

Sue Miller with David Staal

Promiseland is Willow Creek's highly successful children's ministry. Using examples from Promiseland and churches of all sizes around the country, this book provides step-by-step guidance and creative application exercises to help churches develop a thriving children's ministry—one that strives to be the best hour of every kid's week. Included are Scripture-based principles and practical resources for church staff members and volunteers who agree with the critical role children's ministry plays in a local church.

Making Your Children's Ministry the Best Hour of Every Kid's Week, based on twenty-eight years of experience at Willow Creek, explains four ministry foundations: Mission, Vision, Values, and Strategy. Content includes:

- What does Jesus expect from children's ministry?
- How can we evangelize lost kids and disciple saved kids at the same time, and should we?
- How do we engage kids so they don't become bored?
- How do we get better at recruiting and leading volunteers?
- How can our ministry be a safe place for children?
- Six specific ministry values that address the needs of today's children
- Practical first steps for ministries that want to get serious about change
- Clear indicators of success in children's ministry

Softcover: 978-0-310-25485-0

Leading Kids to Jesus

How to Have One-on-One Conversations about Faith

David Staal

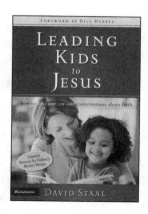

According to a study by George Barna, a person is most likely to become a Christian between the ages of four and fourteen. Yet the majority of evangelism training is designed to reach adults, not children. *Leading Kids to Jesus* equips children's ministry leaders with proven principles to help them have life-changing discussions with kids. The focus is exclusively on personal interactions, not corporate presentations or prop-driven illustrations. Readers learn the best ways to communicate God's love to toddlers, preschoolers, and elementary school children in words they understand. The book adapts two simple communication tools from the bestselling evangelism course Becoming a Contagious Christian, which helps you develop your own three-part story and the four components of the gospel message. Included is a survey of what questions to expect from kids, along with other helps and children's ministry experience from Willow Creek's Promiseland staff and volunteers. A companion volume for parents called *Leading Your Child to Jesus* is also available.

Softcover: 978-0-310-26382-1

Pick up a copy today at your favorite bookstore!

Leading Your Child to Jesus

How Parents Can Talk with Their Kids about Faith

David Staal

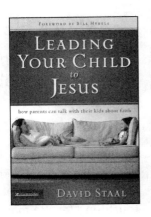

What will you say when your child asks how Jesus can fit inside his heart?

Here's help with responding in words your little one will understand. *Leading Your Child to Jesus* equips you with the simple, effective communication tools that will help you discuss salvation with your child. They've been proven through David Staal's years with Willow Creek Community Church's Promiseland children's ministry and through his personal experiences as a parent.

Learn how to share you own salvation story, explain the gospel in kid-friendly language, and lead your child in a prayer of salvation. Based on examples from the book of Acts, *Leading Your Child to Jesus* provides you with key biblical concepts on effective communication and includes exercises to help you put those concepts into action.

The enormity of leading your child to Christ doesn't have to leave you tongue-tied. You can help your little one make the most important decision of his or her life—the decision to follow Jesus.

Softcover: 978-0-310-26537-5

Pick up a copy today at your favorite bookstore!

Share Your Thoughts

With the Author: Your comments will be forwarded to the author when you send them to *zauthor@zondervan.com*.

With Zondervan: Submit your review of this book by writing to *zreview@zondervan.com*.

Free Online Resources at
www.zondervan.com/hello

 Zondervan AuthorTracker: Be notified whenever your favorite authors publish new books, go on tour, or post an update about what's happening in their lives.

 Daily Bible Verses and Devotions: Enrich your life with daily Bible verses or devotions that help you start every morning focused on God.

 Free Email Publications: Sign up for newsletters on fiction, Christian living, church ministry, parenting, and more.

 Zondervan Bible Search: Find and compare Bible passages in a variety of translations at www.zondervanbiblesearch.com.

 Other Benefits: Register yourself to receive online benefits like coupons and special offers, or to participate in research.